# Wonderful WORLD 6

## PUPIL'S BOOK

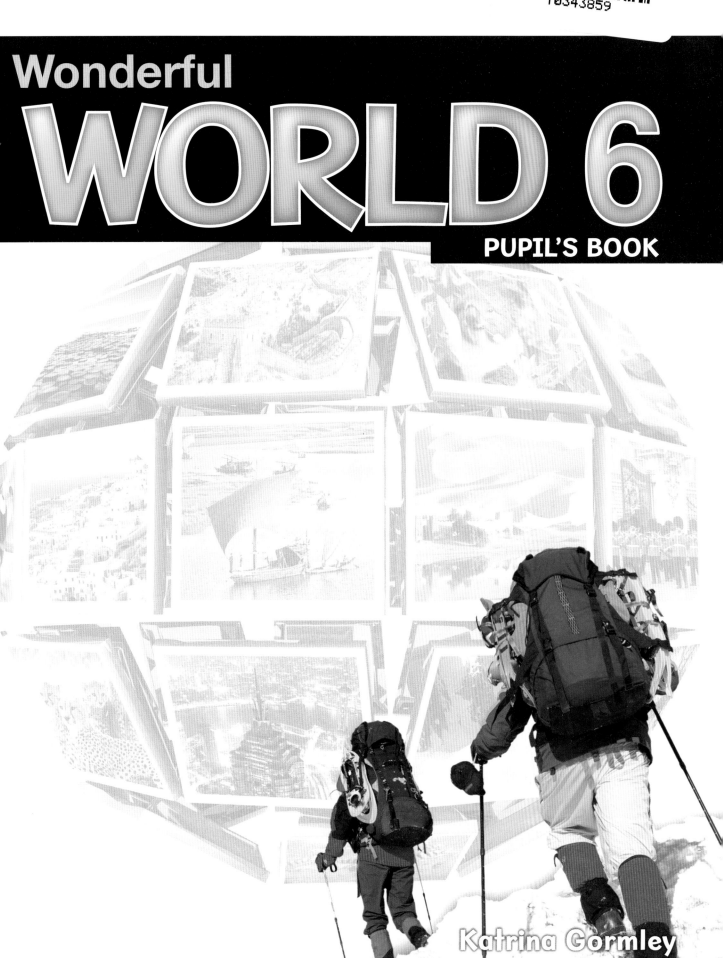

Katrina Gormley

# Contents

| Listening | Speaking | Writing |
|---|---|---|
| Change words in bold<br>Tick correct pictures | Talk about a famous person<br>Talking about people: describe pictures of famous people; talk about being famous | Write about a famous person<br>Register<br>Review |
| Multiple choice<br>Complete notes | Ask and answer questions about museums<br>Opening discussions, Explaining choices: discuss options for learning about history | Write about a museum visit<br>Topic sentences and supporting ideas<br>Essay |
| Number pictures<br>Right or wrong? | Interview about hobbies and pastimes<br>Speculating: describe pictures of people doing their hobbies; talk about which one appeals to you | Write an interview about hobbies<br>Editing<br>Email |
| Multiple matching<br>Tick correct boxes | Ask and answer questions about your area<br>Justifying choices: discuss options for facilities in your area | Write about places<br>Narrative tenses<br>Story |
| Complete a table<br>Multiple matching | Ask and answer questions about a journey<br>Balancing arguments: describe pictures of ways of travelling; talk about means of transport | Write an interview about a journey<br>Adjectives<br>Email of invitation |
| Number issues<br>Tick correct pictures | Talk about making your lifestyle healthier<br>Agreeing, Disagreeing, Conceding a point: discuss options for a healthier lifestyle | Write a short text about lifestyles<br>Capturing and keeping readers' interest<br>Magazine article |
| Tick correct boxes<br>Complete notes | Talk about a country<br>Predicting; describe pictures of environmental problems; talk about what we can do for the environment | Write a fact sheet about a country<br>Linking words and phrases 1<br>Report |
| Change words in bold<br>Tick correct boxes | Ask and answer questions about gadgets<br>Giving advice: discuss technology in young people's lives | Write an advert for a gadget<br>Linking words and phrases 2<br>Email of complaint |
| Circle correct words<br>Right or wrong? | Talk about careers<br>Talking about work, Job titles: describe pictures showing different working conditions | Write about your future career<br>Writing successful stories<br>Story |
| Multiple choice<br>Multiple matching | Talk about pictures showing emergency situations/crimes<br>Giving your opinions, Presenting arguments: discuss adolescent crime | Write a short article about an emergency situation<br>Who, what, where, when, how and why<br>Newspaper article |
| Number pictures<br>Complete notes | Talk about clothes and accessories<br>Describing people (Feelings, size, clothes and appearance): describe pictures showing people; discuss young people's attitude to appearance | Write a description of you're partner's clothes<br>Expressing positive and negative ideas<br>Essay |
| Circle correct words<br>Tick correct pictures | Talk about mysteries, myths and legends<br>Expressing preferences and opinions: discuss suitable mysteries for the school magazine | Write a short story about a mystery, myth or legend<br>Qualifiers<br>Email about a strange event |

# Introduction

This strange-looking bird is known as a blue-footed booby. Its name comes from the Spanish word 'bobo', which means 'silly', because of the clumsy way it walks on land. The booby lives along the coastal areas of the Pacific Ocean and in the Galápagos Islands, an island chain west of Ecuador famous for its unusual species of animals.

## Quiz

Many birds have funny names. Which of the following is actually a real bird?

a   the striped long-neck

b   the spotted thick-knee

c   the tartan brown-belly

# Countable / uncountable nouns

Complete the sentences with the singular or plural of these words.

> application   difference   furniture
> information   suitcase   weight

1 Louise packed lots of _____ for her month-long trip.
2 The company has received a lot of excellent _____ for the job.
3 Her living room was filled with really expensive wooden _____ .
4 The two sisters have got lots of _____, but they get on well.
5 Neil has lost a lot of _____ on his diet.
6 This pamphlet contains lots of _____ on the theme park.

# Describing quantities

Look at the pictures. Use a singular or plural word from column A and a singular or plural word from column B to complete the phrases.

| A | B |
|---|---|
| bottle | bean |
| bowl | coffee |
| can | ketchup |
| cup | noodle |
| glass | olive |
| jar | orange juice |

1 a _____
  of _____

2 two _____
  of _____

3 two _____
  of _____

4 a _____
  of _____

5 two _____
  of _____

6 a _____
  of _____

# Parts of Speech

A Match.

| | | | |
|---|---|---|---|
| 1 | An adjective | a | expresses an action or a state. |
| 2 | A noun | b | describes a noun. |
| 3 | A verb | c | is definite or indefinite. |
| 4 | An adverb | d | is a verb used with another verb. |
| 5 | A preposition | e | is a person, place or thing. |
| 6 | An article | f | is used instead of a noun. |
| 7 | A modal verb | g | adds information to a verb or adjective. |
| 8 | A pronoun | h | is used before a noun to show place, time, etc. |

B Place each word in bold in the table below.

1 This **excellent** restaurant **serves** delicious meals **quickly**.
2 Rebecca wants to meet **a famous archaeologist**.
3 **Everyone must** concentrate **on** protecting **our planet**.
4 **The** journalist **interviewed** the president of **Russia**.
5 **Can** people **communicate easily** with animals?
6 **They often** go shopping **at** the weekend.

| Nouns | Verbs | Adjectives | Adverbs |
|---|---|---|---|
| | | | |
| | | | |
| | | | |

| Pronouns | Prepositions | Modal verbs | Articles |
|---|---|---|---|
| | | | |
| | | | |

# Confusing words

A Circle the correct words.

1 Where do scientists get their / they're amazing ideas?
2 What's the name of the hotel your / you're staying in?
3 This shop has changed it's / its hours of business.
4 'Where's Frank?' 'Maybe / May be he's in the kitchen.'
5 Do you know the man whose / who's in this photo?

B Write out in full the contractions in bold.

1 'Where's Tom?' '**He's** lying down right now.'   _____
2 Mary said **she'd** got a card in the mail.   _____
3 **He'd** go with you if you asked.   _____
4 **It's** been a long time since I've seen you.   _____
5 **There's** some cake in the fridge.   _____
6 **There's** been another earthquake, unfortunately.   _____

## Quiz

**What is the name of the prize given for the best film actors?**

a   Charlie

b   Oscar

c   Bravo

Fame and celebrity have become increasingly important in many countries in recent years. There is an increasing number of TV programmes, books, magazines and internet sites that report on film, TV and pop music celebrities' lives in great detail. Not everyone, though, likes this 'celebrity culture' and not all celebrities enjoy the intense media attention.

# 1 Lesson 1

## Reading

Read the webpage about how to become rich and famous.
What advice does it give to people who make mistakes?

**Discussion**

'Many people spend years trying to get into the public eye, and when they finally succeed they spend all their time trying to hide from the public.' Discuss.

---

**Internet**

Back | Forward | ✗ Stop | Refresh | Home | Search

Address: @ www.stars-r-us.org

# Reach for the Stars!

**So you want to be rich and famous?**
Do you dream of fame and fortune? (1) _____ We all know the road to success is a hard one, but those who are determined succeed. Here are a few tips for readers with stars in their eyes.

**Know your strengths**
Work out what your true talent is and focus on developing it. (2) _____ This is what will win people over and make you stand out from the crowd. You can always work on those dance steps once you've got the attention you need.

**Study the competition**
(3) _____ Newspapers, magazines and websites publish articles on famous people all the time. The stars of the future regularly make time to read what celebrities are doing and make a note of what they do right and what they do wrong.

**Get yourself noticed**
In some ways, it's easy to become well known these days. Television reality shows give ordinary people the chance to show off their talents. (4) _____ The judges don't always choose the contestants who are the best performers; they sometimes select the people who show they can work hard and have lots of potential.

**Learn from your mistakes**
Even the most successful celebrities make mistakes. (5) _____ You are still developing your talent, so recognising when you do something wrong and working to correct it will make you better in the future. Real stars never give up just because they sang a bit off key or slipped during a dance routine. They use this as an opportunity to improve.

**Enjoy yourself**
There's no point in becoming rich and famous if it makes you miserable. The measure of true success is how happy you are when you achieve your goals.

*Good luck on your journey to the top!*

---

## Comprehension

**Complete the webpage with these sentences.**

a  Keep up to date with people who are famous for doing what you do best.

b  Don't be disappointed if this happens to you.

c  If you're a great actor but a lousy dancer then work on your acting.

d  Are you working on becoming the next big hit?

e  Audition for relevant programmes and show how keen you are.

## Vocabulary

**Find the words in the text and circle the correct meaning, a or b.**

1  hard
   a  difficult
   b  firm

2  tip
   a  extra money
   b  piece of advice

3  steps
   a  stairs
   b  movements

4  routine
   a  schedule
   b  performance

5  goals
   a  aims
   b  scores

6  hit
   a  success
   b  slap

# Grammar

## Present Simple and Present Continuous

We use the Present Simple to talk about:
a  facts and general truths.
   *Houses in Beverly Hills cost a fortune.*
b  routines and habits.
   *The band goes on tour every autumn.*
c  permanent states or situations.
   *The British Royal Family lives in Buckingham Palace.*
d  timetabled and programmed events in the future.
   *The concert starts at 8 pm tomorrow.*

### Time expressions

Adverbs of frequency (always, often, usually, regularly, frequently, sometimes, rarely, never), once/twice a week/month, on Thursdays, in July, on April 22nd

We use the Present Continuous to talk about:
a  temporary actions or situations or things happening now.
   *The museum is exhibiting portraits this month.*
b  fixed future plans.
   *I'm interviewing Reese Witherspoon next week.*
c  annoying habits (with always, constantly or forever).
   *That actor is always arguing with his friend.*
d  changing situations.
   *He's becoming richer and richer every year.*
e  what is happening in a picture or photograph.
   *The actor is waving to his fans in this photo.*

### Time expressions

(right) now, at the moment, for the time being, tomorrow, this afternoon/week/winter, next week/month, these days

## A  Circle the correct words.

1  The Millionaire's Club meets / is meeting once a week.
2  We're not flying / don't fly to Monaco tomorrow.
3  This newspaper is printing / prints gossip every day.
4  Does he break / Is he breaking the glasses often?
5  Do you read / Are you reading a biography at the moment?

## B  Complete the postcard with the Present Simple or the Present Continuous of these verbs.

| have   get up   go   show   stay |

Hi Alexandra and Joanna,

How are you? I (1) _____ in a hotel in Beverly Hills. It's amazing! I (2) _____ and go down for breakfast and then I (3) _____ for a swim in the pool. There's always a celebrity there. It's so cool!
Later today, the hotel (4) _____ some films and TV programmes that have been made here. After that, some directors (5) _____ a huge party for stars and hotel guests. I'm so excited!

Love to you both,

Sasha

# Word formation

## A  Complete the table.

| Verb | Noun | Adjective |
|------|------|-----------|
| (1) _____ | success | successful |
| achieve | (2) _____ | achievable |
| determine | determination | (3) _____ |
| (4) _____ | competition | competitive |
| impress | impression | (5) _____ |
| admire | (6) _____ | admirable |

## B  Complete the sentences with some of the words from A.

1  I'm full of _____ for the winners of the children's talent competition.
2  You have to try hard to _____ as an actor.
3  Some people are _____ to become rich and famous.
4  I didn't make a good _____ at the audition.
5  Winning the music award is my greatest _____ so far.
6  How many contestants will _____ in the talent show?

# Speaking

**Work with a partner. Take it in turns to tell each other about a famous person you admire. Use these phrases to help you.**

He/She is a famous …
He/She lives in …
He/She is (nationality)/twenty-eight years old/talented/etc.
He/She likes/dislikes …

# Writing

**Write a short paragraph about the person you told your partner about in the Speaking task.**

## Discussion

Imagine you are super-rich. What object belonging to a famous person would you buy?

## Reading

**Read the article below. What did someone buy for 87,000 dollars?**

# All you need is a lot of spare cash!

Collecting celebrities' memorabilia appears to be a very popular, but very extravagant, pastime these days. Some people just love the possessions of the rich and famous. Many are even willing to hand over huge sums of money at auctions to purchase goods which their favourite star owns or has used. It seems that even higher amounts are paid when the owner is no longer alive.

In August 2000 at an auction in Indiana, USA, a car which was driven by former Beatle John Lennon was put up for auction. Lennon, who died in 1980 and who had an extremely successful solo career with tracks such as *Imagine* and *Woman*, designed the stunning paintwork on the luxury car. Thousands of people turned up in Indiana on the day the 1956 Bentley appeared at the auction. The car was sold for an impressive 325,000 dollars. That's a lot of money for an old car, but some people

believe it's worth it. Today, *Beatles*, Lennon and vintage car enthusiasts flock to the Sarasota Car Museum in Florida to see the car on display.

Genuine celebrity clothes are also in great demand at auctions and wealthy fans often pay an arm and a leg for clothes that they want. Take a look at these examples: a leather jacket worn on stage by U2's lead singer Bono fetched over 37,000 dollars, while a jacket former *Nirvana* singer Kurt Cobain wore while performing went for 87,000 dollars.

Do you think these prices are outrageous and these buyers are crazy? You're probably right, but stars' possessions are often snapped up by museums which exhibit these items for the general public to see. That way more people get a glimpse of stardom.

## Comprehension

**Write A if the sentence is correct and B if it is not correct.**

1 Collecting rich and famous people's possessions is an inexpensive hobby.
2 A car used by John Lennon was sold at an auction in 1980.
3 The car used by Lennon is now part of a car museum exhibition.
4 Bono's leather jacket was bought for 87,000 dollars.
5 Celebrities' memorabilia is often bought by museums.

### Guess what!

In 2009, a glove that was tossed to an Australian fan by Michael Jackson at a concert in 1996 was sold to a hotel in Las Vegas for more than £29,000!

# Vocabulary

**Circle the correct words.**

1 Many pop stars drive expensive vintage / former cars.
2 Which track / auction do you like best from this CD?
3 The Solid Rock Museum displays all sorts of rock paintwork / memorabilia.
4 Many music fans want to get a glimpse / look of their favourite stars.
5 Most singers try to look stunning / extravagant on stage.
6 It's absolutely genuine / outrageous how much he spends every week.

# Grammar

## Stative verbs

We don't usually use verbs which describe states (stative verbs) in continuous tenses. Stative verbs include verbs that refer to feelings, possession, opinion and understanding, state of mind and the senses.

*I really like this DVD.*
*This villa belongs to a millionaire.*
*I doubt the band's next track will be a hit.*

Some verbs can be either stative or non-stative with different meanings. These verbs include be, think, feel, appear, see and have.

*It appears that a fan bought the celebrity's motorbike.*
*How many bands are appearing at the festival this year?*

**Complete the sentences using the Present Simple or the Present Continuous of the verbs in brackets.**

1 The bank manager _____ (see) the billionaire this morning.
2 Many young people _____ (want) to be rich and famous.
3 Why _____ (he / taste) your food?
4 The lead singer _____ (hate) fans coming to rehearsals.
5 The singer _____ (think) of going on tour.
6 Iris _____ (doubt) her latest film will be a success.
7 The famous couple _____ (have) a holiday on a remote island at the moment.
8 Why _____ (people / love) reading about Hollywood actors?

# Vocabulary

**Choose the correct answers.**

1 The Tutankhamun treasures are on _____ at the Egyptian Museum in Cairo.
  a display      b auction      c demand
2 *Rush's* new CD is now on _____ .
  a loan      b sale      c purchase
3 Who's appearing on _____ at the Apollo this weekend?
  a show      b exhibit      c stage
4 The fans were out of _____ at the concert.
  a control      b fortune      c action
5 Did you get a _____ of your favourite actor at the premiere?
  a look      b glimpse      c sight

# Listening

🎧 **Listen to the interview with Janice Porter and change the words in bold to make the sentences true.**

1 Janice was Gary Allen's **mother**. _____
2 This is the **third** interview Janice has given since Gary died. _____
3 The auction will take place next **month**. _____
4 *Hanging Garden* split up in **2010**. _____
5 The record company should **sell** the memorabilia to a museum. _____

## Phrasal Verbs

**Complete the sentences with these words.**

| go for | hand over | head for |
|---|---|---|
| snap up | split up | turn up |

1 How much did Bono's leather jacket _____ in the sale?
2 Tom's disappointed because his favourite band is going to _____ .
3 How many fans are expected to _____ at the memorial?
4 As soon as filming stops many actors _____ exotic islands for a holiday.
5 Come on! _____ the keys to my Bentley!
6 Josh wants to _____ his favourite star's costume at the auction.

## Vocabulary

**A  Circle the odd one out.**

| | | | |
|---|---|---|---|
| 1 | signed copy | autograph | charity |
| 2 | glamorous | former | stunning |
| 3 | sequel | premiere | opening |
| 4 | millionaire | TV guide | front cover |
| 5 | champion | star | orphan |
| 6 | poverty-stricken | familiar | well known |

**B  Complete the sentences using some of the words from Task A.**

1  I enjoyed the _____ more than the first movie.

2  Unfortunately, Rachel doesn't have any parents. She's a(n) _____ .

3  That star works for a(n) _____ that helps children in need.

4  He's not poverty-stricken but he's not a(n) _____ either.

5  This model has been on the _____ of several magazines.

6  The house where I live is the _____ home of a film star.

## Listening skills

**A  Work with a partner and discuss the differences between the two sets of pictures below.**

**B  Listen to the two dialogues and tick (✓) the correct boxes to answer these questions.**

1  What is the man showing the girls?

2  Who do the children see on the boat?

**C  Now work with a partner to discuss your answers and say why the other pictures are wrong.**

## Listening task

🎧 **Listen and tick (✓) the correct pictures.**

1  How much does the T-shirt cost?

2  How is the actor travelling to the film premiere?

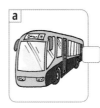  

3  What does the fan win in the competition?

 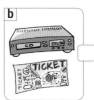 

4  What is the guitarist doing?

5  What is on sale at the auction?

6  What day is it today?

**Talking about people**

It/He/She looks like …

It/He/She seems/appears to be + -ing

I (don't) think/believe/imagine he/she …

He/She is wearing/looking at/playing …

# Listen Up!

🎧 **Listen to Sakis and Eleni doing the speaking task below. Make a note of what each student does right or wrong and of any appropriate language they use.**

*Work with a partner and take it in turns to describe what you can see in these pictures. Student A should talk about picture 1 and Student B should talk about picture 2.*

# Speaking skills

**A** Tick (✓) the most polite reply to these questions.

1 What do you think of the band's performance?
   a It's terrible. They're totally useless and shouldn't be on stage.
   b It could be better. I imagine they're feeling very nervous.

2 What's your opinion of Amy's new hairstyle?
   a To be honest, I don't think it suits her.
   b She's done it like that for a joke, hasn't she?

3 What do you think of the lead singer's dress?
   a It's very glamorous, but she appears to be uncomfortable in it.
   b It's obviously meant for someone half her age.

**B** Work with a partner and role play an interview with a music fan. Student A is a fan at a concert and Student B is a journalist for a music magazine. Use the expressions from *Express Yourself!* and the dialogues in A to help you. Try to be polite!

# Speaking tasks

**A** Read the task in B and tick the items which describe what you have to do.

1 describe what the people in the picture look like ☐
2 say where the picture has been taken ☐
3 describe the people's clothes ☐
4 decide which picture you both like best ☐
5 say what the people are doing ☐
6 guess what happens next ☐
7 talk about your partner's picture ☐
8 describe every object in the picture ☐

**B** Work with a partner and take it in turns to describe what you can see in these pictures. Student A should talk about picture 1 and Student B should talk about picture 2.

**C** Now talk to your partner about what you would like to be famous for and what you imagine your life would be like as a famous person.

13

## Register

 Before we begin writing something, we must decide which register is appropriate. For example, postcards, emails and friendly letters should use informal language; reviews and articles are usually written in semi-formal language, and job applications and letters of complaint should be formal.

**Read these sentences and tick (✓) the ones that are appropriate for a semi-formal review. Why are the others not appropriate?**

1  The only word I can find for the story is stupid. ☐

2  The plot of the film is simple. ☐

3  The film is neither a complete failure nor a huge success. ☐

4  Even a five-year-old could act better than these actors. ☐

5  This film is utter rubbish. ☐

6  The actors don't fulfil their potential. ☐

## Writing task

**A  Read this writing task and answer the questions.**

*Write a review of a film you have seen for your school magazine. Describe what happens in the film and say what you liked about it and what you didn't like about it.*

1  What type of text will you write?

2  Will you only write positive things about the film?

3  Who will read the review?

4  What three things will your review include?

**B  Circle the correct words to complete the model review.**

*model composition*

# My Life in Ruins

The 2009 Tribeca Film Festival closed with a film premiere that many expected to be better. The comedy *My Life in Ruins* isn't (1) a complete flop / absolute rubbish, but nor is it a huge hit.

The main weakness of the film is the plot, which is fairly (2) predictable / dim-witted. A tour guide (Nia Vardalos) lives an extremely boring life. Every day she shows tourists cultural sights. She becomes disappointed because she always seems to have (3) idiots / tourists who are not interested in ancient ruins. Everything always seems to go wrong with hilarious cultural and personality clashes.

The real star of this film is the set. Some scenes take place in the stunning Parthenon. The Greek government allowed filming here for *My Life in Ruins* so film audiences all over the world can get a glimpse of this admirable monument. As far as the cast is concerned, the local actor Alexis Georgoulis (4) steals the limelight from / is loads better than the film's star Nia Vardalos.

Overall, *My Life in Ruins* (5) is a complete waste of time / doesn't fulfil its potential, but the scenery is (6) very impressive / not too bad. Producers made the film hoping to repeat the success of Vardalos' 2002 film *My Big Fat Greek Wedding*. Critics are unlikely to give this film as much praise as that one received, but it will be in great demand with fans of Greece and Georgoulis.

# Analyse it!

**Answer these questions.**

1  What is the main tense used in the model review?
2  Why is this tense used?
3  What are the film's negative points?
4  What are the film's positive points?
5  Are the answers you circled in the model review polite or impolite?

# Writing plan

**Complete the plan for the model review with these points.**

a  give your overall impression of the film and say who it appeals to
b  introduce the film you are going to review
c  narrate the plot of the film
d  say what the film's negative points are
e  say what the film's positive points are

Paragraph 1  _____
Paragraph 2  _____
Paragraph 3  _____
Paragraph 4  _____

# Grammar

### Direct and indirect objects

Some sentences have two objects. The direct object is the person, animal or thing to which the verb relates or the action is done. The indirect object is the person, animal or thing which can receive the direct object or to whom the direct object is given. The indirect object always comes before the direct object. Verbs which can take two objects are usually verbs of communication or giving such as send, offer, lend, take, tell, sell, buy, bring, show and give.

*The singer gave James his autograph.*
*Helen bought everyone tickets.*

We can also write these sentences using a prepositional phrase with to or for.
*The singer gave his autograph to James.*
*Helen bought tickets for everyone.*

## A  Match.

| | |
|---|---|
| 1  Jason sold the customer | a  for all my friends. |
| 2  Will he tell you | b  your Muse CD? |
| 3  Will you lend me | c  his secret? |
| 4  The singer brought drinks | d  three tickets. |
| 5  I'll send a letter | e  to Mum. |

## B  Look at the sentences highlighted in the model review and answer the questions.

1  Which are the direct and the indirect objects?
2  How can we rewrite these sentences?

# Writing task

*Write a review of a film which you really enjoyed for a magazine. Describe what happens in the film and discuss two features that particularly impressed you.*

## Write right!

**Use these steps to help you write your review.**

**Step 1**  Underline the points in the Writing task that you must include in your review.
**Step 2**  Choose a film you really enjoyed.
**Step 3**  Research and make notes about the film's plot, the characters, the setting and any other impressive features.
**Step 4**  Make a plan for your review. Make sure it has an introduction, two or three middle paragraphs and a conclusion. Use the plan opposite to help you.
**Step 5**  Use your notes, your plan and the useful language above to write your review.

## Discussion

'Hollywood actors earn far too much money.' Discuss.

# 2 History

## Quiz

**Who built the city of Petra?**

a   the Romans
b   the Nabataeans
c   the Greeks

The city of Petra is one of the most important and beautiful cities from the ancient world. No one knows exactly when it was founded, but archaeologists believe it was about 2,500 years ago. It was built by people from what is now Saudi Arabia and it was an important trading centre in ancient times. The buildings show Greek, Egyptian and Syrian influences. All the monuments we see today were carved from steep red-coloured cliffs which have given Petra its name, the Rose City.

Petra declined under Roman rule and a serious earthquake destroyed many of the buildings and the city's water channels in 363.

The city was forgotten about in Western culture until 1812 when the Swiss explorer Johann Ludwig Burchardt 'rediscovered' it.

Petra has been a UNESCO World Heritage Site since 1985 and is Jordan's most famous and treasured tourist attraction.

## Lesson 1

**Discussion**

In what ways do you think life was different for people of your age:

a fifty years ago?

b in ancient times?

## Reading

**Read the story about Rebecca's trip to a museum. In what ways is she similar to the girl who lived in Victorian times? In what way is she different?**

# Portrait of a journalist

When she arrived at the museum, Rebecca didn't quite know what to expect. She suspected the curator had seen her newspaper article with the photos of museum exhibits she had taken, which weren't very good.

'The museum's closed, Miss,' the guard uttered in a tired voice.

'But I have an appointment with the curator at 7.30,' Rebecca said, puzzled.

'Who? Mrs Watts? Well, you'd better go in then.'

Rebecca pushed open the heavy wooden door and immediately came face to face with Mrs Watts.

'Ah, you're Rebecca, aren't you?' she said. 'Come this way, please.'

Their footsteps echoed on the stone floor as they were walking through the exhibition halls. Rebecca was beginning to feel uneasy when suddenly the curator stopped in front of an old trunk.

'I was researching the history of a new exhibit last week,' she said. 'It's this trunk from 1867. It belonged to a young girl called Eliza who wanted to become a journalist. Unfortunately, Victorian society didn't approve of such a profession for a girl. She was expected to marry and have children. Her trunk contained a diary, and I also found this.'

Mrs Watts took a scroll out of the trunk and handed it to Rebecca. When she looked at it, Rebecca went as white as a sheet. It was a portrait of a girl who looked exactly like her.

'But who was she?' Rebecca asked in amazement.

'That's the interesting part,' said the curator. 'I was on my way to your newspaper's offices on Monday to complain about your use of photos of museum exhibits. But you were leaving the building just as I arrived. I was very surprised when I saw your face. I rushed back to the museum and did more research. It turns out that Eliza was your ancestor.'

Rebecca was speechless. She realised how lucky she was that, unlike Eliza, her dreams had come true; she had always wanted to be a journalist and she had become one. She couldn't wait to find out more. She was thinking about the story she could write about Eliza when suddenly the curator spoke again.

'Now, I'm sure you have lots of questions, but about those photos ...,' she said with a smile on her face.

## Comprehension

**Answer the questions.**

1 How do we know Rebecca has been to the museum before?

2 Who is Mrs Watts?

3 Which word tells us that Rebecca was nervous while she was walking through the museum?

4 How did Rebecca feel when she saw the portrait?

5 What makes Rebecca feel lucky?

## Vocabulary

**Find words in the story that have these meanings. The words are in the same order as they appear in the text.**

1 person in charge of museum exhibits  _____

2 said  _____

3 confused  _____

4 worried  _____

5 think something is suitable  _____

6 long roll of paper  _____

# Grammar

## Past Simple and Past Continuous

We use the Past Simple for actions that started and finished in the past; for actions that happened one after the other in the past; and for past habits.
*The museum didn't put any new exhibits on display this year.*
*They arrived at the site, found their tools and started digging.*
*Did children play games in medieval times?*

We use the Past Continuous for actions that were in progress at a specific time in the past; for two or more actions that were happening at the same time in the past; and to set the scene of a story.
*Rea was writing about Ancient Egypt last night.*
*I was watching a film and my brother was sleeping.*
*It was getting cold and dark at the archaeological site.*

## as, when, while

We can use the Past Simple and the Past Continuous in the same sentence to show that one action interrupted another in the past or to tell a story. We usually use as, when and while to connect the two actions. As and while usually come before the Past Continuous and when usually comes before the Past Simple.
*As/While they were entering the pyramid, it started to rain heavily.*
*They were visiting the Natural History Museum when the earthquake happened.*

## A Choose the correct answers.

1 The *Mary Rose* _____ in 1545.
   a  sunk
   b  sank
   c  was sinking

2 The curator _____ any new exhibits last season.
   a  did she purchase
   b  wasn't purchasing
   c  didn't purchase

3 Why was _____ under an apple tree?
   a  Isaac Newton sat
   b  Isaac Newton sitting
   c  did Isaac Newton sit

4 As _____ her history project, her mum called.
   a  Karen finished
   b  Karen was finishing
   c  did Karen finish

5 I was reading about lost civilizations _____ the lights went out.
   a  as
   b  while
   c  when

6 Where was Costas digging when he _____ across the bones?
   a  came
   b  come
   c  was coming

## B Complete the text with the Past Simple or the Past Continuous of the verbs in brackets.

Christopher Columbus and Ibn Battuta are famous throughout the world for their sea voyages, but Chinese admiral Zheng He is not so well-known. Zheng He (1) _____ (set off) on his travels in 1405 to explore the world. He was the leader of fleets with over 300 ships and 30,000 sailors. These ships (2) _____ (carry) Chinese silk and other goods and Zheng He traded them for goods from other countries. While he (3) _____ (travel), he visited many countries in Asia and Africa and he (4) _____ (introduce) the people there to Chinese culture. Zheng He went on seven world voyages in total, but he (5) _____ (not make) it back from his last one. He died in 1433 as he (6) _____ (sail) back to China from the east coast of Africa.

## Collocations

**Circle the correct words.**

1 Visiting the Pyramids was a dream come real / true.

2 Alice came face to face / neck and neck with a dinosaur skeleton in the museum.

3 World War II came to an end / a finish in 1945.

4 Civilization has come a long path / way since medieval times.

5 When did Julius Caesar come to power / rule?

6 It came as no amazement / surprise that Hillary failed her history exam.

# Speaking

**Work with a partner. Take it in turns to ask and answer these questions.**

When was the last time you visited a museum?

What exhibit impressed you the most?

Why did you find it impressive?

Was there anything you didn't find impressive? Why?

# Writing

**Write a short email to a friend telling him/her about a visit to a museum. Use your answers to the questions in the Speaking task to help you.**

## Lesson 2

**Discussion**

'History can't teach us anything useful.' Discuss.

## Reading

Read the article about Skara Brae. How many Neolithic houses can you see at Skara Brae today?

# Skara Brae – a window on the past

The Orkney Islands off the northern coast of mainland Scotland face harsh winters with heavy storms. In the winter of 1850, such a storm hit the southern shore of the Bay of Skaill, marking a turning point for the island and its heritage.

The storm removed layers of grass and sand from a hill on the beach at the Bay of Skaill and the outline of buildings became visible. This led to the first excavation of the site and the remains of four stone houses were revealed. The site remained in this condition from 1868 until 1925 when another storm uncovered more structures. A second excavation took place between 1928 and 1930 and brought the village to its present state with eight houses linked by winding tunnels, probably used by villagers to get from one house to another without going outside. In the 1970s, tests confirmed that the settlement is Neolithic and that the village used to be inhabited five thousand years ago.

The houses and most of their furniture are very well preserved because the villagers used to build with stone instead of wood. The houses were approximately the same size and shape and most of them had the same basic design. There was one room with a fireplace in the middle, where villagers would cook their food, and stone beds on either side. However, two of the buildings are different. House Seven is a building with its own entrance which locks from the outside and is detached from the others. People have suggested that this building was either a jail or the place where women used to give birth, but nobody really knows. House Eight, on the other hand, was probably the place where the inhabitants would gather together.

While the purpose of these buildings is uncertain, Skara Brae's biggest mystery is why the inhabitants left the village. One theory says they left suddenly due to fear of a natural disaster. Another simply suggests that Neolithic life began to change and younger people migrated to different areas to live and work, leaving only the older villagers at the settlement. In time, they passed away and Skara Brae fell silent. 34

## Comprehension

**The words in bold are wrong. Write the correct words.**

1  Ruins at Skara Brae were discovered in **1868** and **1928**.  _____

2  The **first** excavation ended in 1930.  _____

3  Tests confirmed that the village was inhabited **in the 1970s**.  _____

4  The inhabitants built with **wood**.  _____

5  The word 'Another' in line 34 refers to another **mystery**.  _____

**Guess what!**

The period before the Neolithic period – the Palaeolithic, also known as the New Stone Age (4,000–6,000 years ago), is the time when people first started farming and stopped being nomadic.

20

# Vocabulary

Complete the sentences with these words.

| confirm | face | migrate |
|---------|------|---------|
| preserved | visible | winding |

1 There is a _____ path next to the site.
2 People had to _____ difficult living conditions in the past.
3 It's amazing how well _____ these old buildings are.
4 Much of Cairo is _____ from the Al Azhar Park.
5 Archaeologists can _____ the settlement was very small.
6 People would often _____ from one place to another in the past.

# Grammar

## Used to and Would

We use used to + bare infinitive to talk about actions that happened often in the past but no longer happen and to talk about states that existed in the past but no longer exist.
*In Neolithic times, people used to build houses out of stone.*
*My ancestors used to live in Portugal.*

> **Note:** We can use didn't use to to talk about actions or states that happen often or exist now but that didn't in the past.
> *People on the Orkney Islands didn't use to know that Skara Brae existed.* (But they do now.)

We use would to talk about actions that happened often in the past but no longer happen. We can't use would to talk about states in the past, and we don't use usually the negative form (wouldn't).
*In the evenings, they would gather round the fireplace.*

**A** **Look back at the highlighted phrases in the article. Which example of used to could be replaced by would? Why could the other example not be replaced by would?**

**B** **Tick (✓) the sentences which are correct and rewrite the ones which are incorrect with used to or would.**

1 I wouldn't like history when I was at school.
2 Did you used be an archaeologist?
3 People used to buy salt in the market at Timbuktu.
4 The ancient Egyptians used to built pyramids.
5 Would dinosaurs eat anything they found?

# Vocabulary

Complete the word groups.

| inhabitants | millennium |
|-------------|-----------|
| remains | settlement    theory |

1 relics          ruins          _____
2 decade          century        _____
3 idea            suggestion     _____
4 residents       villagers      _____
5 community       neighbourhood  _____

# Listening

🎧 **Do the quiz, then listen and check your answers.**

1 What is the circle of standing stones in southern England called?
a Stonehenge
b Hadrian's Wall
c Nelson's Column

2 When did the first modern Olympic Games take place?
a 776 BC
b 2004
c 1896

3 Which place is not a UNESCO World Heritage Site?
a The ancient city of Petra in Jordan
b The Tower of Hercules in Spain
c Loch Ness in Scotland

4 When did homo erectus first appear on earth?
a almost two million years ago
b over three million years ago
c nearly four thousand years ago

5 Where was Christopher Columbus from?
a Latin America
b Spain
c Italy

## Prepositions

Complete the sentences with these words.

| for | in | of | on | to | with |
|-----|-----|-----|-----|-----|------|

1 The discovery of a pot led _____ a full excavation.
2 We associate these seas _____ pirates.
3 Storms resulted _____ the destruction of the site.
4 What did you base your theory _____?
5 The chief didn't approve _____ the changes.
6 We aren't going to pay _____ further research.

## Vocabulary

Write the correct words.

> costume   exhibition   expert   fighter plane
> finds   fossil   refreshments   skeleton

_____

_____

_____

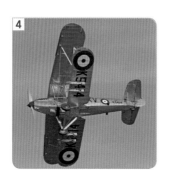

_____

_____

_____

_____

_____

## Listening skills

**A** Look at notes 1–4 in B and match them to these question words.

What? ☐
Where? ☐
How much? ☐
When? ☐

**B** 🎧 Listen to the dialogues and complete the notes.

1. Day of history test: _____
2. Price of DVD: _____
3. History Museum event: Neolithic _____
4. Peruvian exhibits on: _____ floor

## Listening task

🎧 Listen to the information about the Millennium Museum and complete the notes.

### Millennium Museum

**Opening hours:** Daily from 10 am – 6 pm, (1) _____ closed

**Price:** free for general entry; (2) £ _____ for temporary exhibitions

**This season's temporary exhibition:** *Dinosaur World* including T-rex (3) _____ with almost 50% dinosaur remains

**Exhibition of the month:** (4) _____ of World War II fighter planes

**Times of special events:** Talks at (5) _____; films at 1 pm

**Refreshments:** on the (6) _____ floor in the Dickens Café

**Opening discussions**

Let's begin/start by looking at …

First of all, …

To begin with …

**Explaining choices**

I (don't) think/believe … is important/helpful because …

He/She should(n't) … because …

It's a good/not such a good idea to … because …

It'd be better to (if he/she) … because …

# Listen Up!

**A** 🎧 **Listen to Sakis and Eleni discussing which exhibitions to visit at a museum and complete the sentences.**

*Look at these pictures of museum exhibitions and talk about which ones you would like to go to and which ones you wouldn't like to go to.*

1 _____ we should say what each exhibition is.

2 _____ the train exhibition is important because it's only got old means of transport.

3 _____ go to the clothes exhibition because it's got amazing costumes.

4 _____ to go there first because it's a big exhibition.

**B** 🎧 **Listen again. What mistakes do the speakers make with syntax and grammar?**

# Speaking skills

**A** **Look at the pictures in B of possible items to include in an exhibition on World Heritage (1-5). Decide which of these statements you could use to describe each object and write the appropriate number(s) on the lines.**

It takes up too much space. _____

It's not interesting enough. _____

It will attract many visitors. _____

It won't be at all popular. _____

It's in a good condition. _____

Visitors can learn a lot from it. _____

**B** **Imagine that you and your partner are museum curators. Discuss which exhibits to include in an exhibition on World Heritage. Use some of the expressions from A.**

# Speaking tasks

**A friend of yours is going on a tour of Egypt and wants to learn about its ancient history before he or she goes. Look at the pictures and work with a partner to discuss the best ways he can get the information he wants.**

## Topic sentences and supporting ideas

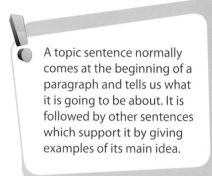

A topic sentence normally comes at the beginning of a paragraph and tells us what it is going to be about. It is followed by other sentences which support it by giving examples of its main idea.

**Look at the topic sentence and tick the sentences that present ideas to support it.**

*In my opinion, the Rosetta Stone belongs in the Egyptian Museum in Cairo and not in the British Museum.*

1 They are an important part of Egyptian history so they should be displayed in Egypt. ☐

2 This will allow people to see it. ☐

3 Also, visitors will be able to appreciate it more if it is among similar exhibits from ancient Egypt. ☐

4 In addition, it's easier to travel to the Egyptian Museum. ☐

5 Moreover, it is over 2,000 years old and it need to be protected. ☐

6 Furthermore, I believe finds belong in their country of origin, so it should never have gone to Britain in the first place. ☐

# Writing task

**A Read the writing task and tick (✓) the sentence that best rephrases the idea in the statement.**

*'Governments should preserve all archaeological finds.' Write an essay based on this statement and say whether you agree or disagree with the opinion it expresses.*

1 Preserving archaeological finds is the main responsibility of governments. ☐

2 Governments haven't always kept all archaeological finds. ☐

3 The authorities must keep and protect the most important finds from archaeological digs. ☐

4 Every archaeological find is valuable and the authorities should protect it. ☐

**B Now read the model essay and complete it with these topic sentences.**

a However, it is impossible to decide which objects are not valuable.

b In conclusion, I believe all archaeological finds are valuable.

c Many people argue that ancient objects are important, but that we do not need to keep every find.

d These days, governments spend large sums of money on archaeological excavations and on preserving archaeological finds.

*model composition*

## To preserve or not to preserve?

(1) _____ The question is should they preserve all finds?

(2) _____ They say that there are so many objects that it's impossible to store everything. Furthermore, they make the point that people can become so used to seeing archaeological remains that they no longer pay attention to them. As a result, they feel that we should keep only the most important objects.

(3) _____ Archaeologists say all finds play a very important part in learning what life was like in the past. Even a very small object can show us how people used to live and how their societies worked. Moreover, archaeologists might not realise how significant an object is immediately. If they do not keep it, then they may lose a piece of a larger puzzle.

(4) _____ We should preserve them as future finds may show us how they link to the past.

# Analyse it!

**Write T (true) or F (false).**

1 The writer has to agree with the statement in the task. ☐

2 The first paragraph rephrases the statement in the task. ☐

3 Each paragraph has got a topic sentence. ☐

4 Paragraph 2 presents arguments that don't support the statement. ☐

5 Paragraph 3 presents arguments that the writer disagrees with. ☐

6 The writer states his/her opinion in all paragraphs. ☐

7 The essay is written in formal language. ☐

# Writing plan

**Complete the plan for the model essay with these words.**

> arguments against     arguments in favour of
> conclusion     opinion     statement

Paragraph 1   Introduce and rephrase the (1) _____ in the task.

Paragraph 2   Present and analyse the (2) _____ the statement.

Paragraph 3   Present and analyse the (3) _____ the statement.

Paragraph 4   Come to a (4) _____ and express your (5) _____ .

# Grammar

## used to, get used to, be used to

We use used to + bare infinitive to talk about actions or states that happened often or existed in the past but don't now.
*I used to walk past an archaeological site on my way to school.*

We use get used to + -ing or a noun to talk about actions or states that are becoming familiar to us. We can use get used to with all tenses and with modal verbs.
*Ingrid is getting used to working as a guide at Skara Brae.*

We use be used to + -ing or a noun to talk about actions or states that no longer seem strange, but that were in the past. We can use be used to with all tenses apart from the continuous tenses and modal verbs.
*Bob must be used to listening to talks on dinosaurs.*

**Complete the second sentence in each pair using the correct form of used to, get used to or be used to.**

1 I hated studying history at school.
  I _____ hate studying history at school.

2 It will be easy for Joe to study history when he's older.
  Joe will _____ studying history when he's older.

3 Our history teacher always gave us good marks.
  Our history teacher always _____ give us good marks.

4 By 1920, cars were becoming a familiar sight to people.
  By 1920, people _____ seeing cars.

5 Sea voyages would last for years in Columbus' time.
  Sea voyages _____ last for years in Columbus' time.

# useful language

**Stating your opinion**
In my opinion/view, …
To my mind, …
I believe/think …

**Giving more examples**
Also, …                    Moreover, …
In addition, …            Furthermore, …

**Comparing/contrasting**
However, …
On the other hand, …

**Concluding**
To sum up, …
In conclusion, …

# Writing task

*'The classroom is the best place to learn about history.' Write an essay based on this statement and say whether you agree or disagree with the opinion it expresses.*

## Write right!

**Use these steps to help you write your essay.**

**Step 1**  Make a note of at least two arguments that support the statement and two that don't support it.

**Step 2**  Decide how you feel about the statement. Do you agree or disagree?

**Step 3**  Research the topic if you feel you need more information before writing.

**Step 4**  Order your ideas in a logical way to plan your essay. Use the plan above to help you.

**Step 5**  Use your notes, your plan and the useful language above to write your essay.

## Discussion

If you could travel back in time, which period in history would you choose to visit? Why? Which period wouldn't you visit? Why not?

# Review 1

## Vocabulary

**A** Write the correct words.

> auction    paintwork    routine
> ruins    settlement    trunk

**B** Circle the correct words.

1 Archaeologists found the fossil / relic of a dinosaur in this area.

2 An ancestor / A heritage of mine was a famous writer.

3 When did they migrate / head for another region?

4 Nobody confirmed / uttered a word during the history lecture.

5 He's a millionaire but he came from a(n) extravagant / poverty-stricken family.

6 Please don't be so competitive / visible.

**C** Use the words in capitals at the end of some of the lines to form words that fit in the gaps.

## Premiere with a cause

The rich and famous usually turn up
to film premieres wearing the most
(1) _____ clothes money can buy.  **GLAMOUR**
They don't want to disappoint the fans
who wait for hours to catch a glimpse of
them as they walk down the red carpet.
However, the (2) _____ of  **OPEN**
Franz Meister's new film was attended
by stars wearing everyday clothes.
Everyone had made an (3) _____  **ADMIRE**
attempt to dress as if the event was
nothing special. The reason for this was
to raise money for the charity *Kids on the
Streets*. The money that is normally
spent on the (4) _____ clothes  **CELEBRATE**
was given to the charity instead.
Some of the stars looked
(5) _____ as they walked down  **EASY**
the red carpet in jeans and T-shirts,
but when it was announced that
(6) _____ five million dollars  **APPROXIMATE**
would go to the charity, they all said it
was worth it. A journalist who was
present at the event made the
(7) _____ that this should  **SUGGEST**
happen more often. She also said it's
(8) _____ how much money  **OUTRAGE**
some stars spend on clothes.

**D** Choose the correct answers.

1 Janice _____ up a vintage watch at an auction.
   a put        b snapped        c turned

2 The President has been in _____ since 1995.
   a power      b potential      c appointment

3 The _____ of this village migrated gradually.
   a curators   b inhabitants    c experts

4 We _____ this area with stories of pirates.
   a associate  b impress        c flock

5 I paid an arm and a _____ for those tickets.
   a face       b footstep       c leg

6 Wow! Is this really a _____ find from the site?
   a genuine    b lousy          c pathetic

## Grammar

**A Match.**

| | |
|---|---|
| 1 The exhibition doesn't | a notice the missing scroll. |
| 2 Tonight the band | b found the bones. |
| 3 Cheryl isn't | c be super-rich. |
| 4 I was digging here when I | d open until Monday. |
| 5 The celebrity used to | e watching a movie now. |
| 6 The curator didn't | f are signing autographs. |

**B Circle the correct answers.**

1 I used / am getting used to living below the museum.

2 George Clooney gave to me / me his autograph.

3 Some celebrities feel / are feeling they can do anything.

4 Dad was a boy when / as they made the first mobile phone.

5 When did this civilization come / coming to an end?

6 Our history teacher would / used to be an archaeologist.

**C Write sentences with these words and make any changes necessary to the verb forms.**

1 Robin / buy / a signed copy of the CD / last week

2 they / attend / a film premiere / at the moment

3 ? / she / give / the relic / to you / yesterday

4 the dinosaur skeleton / be / now / on display

5 I / look for / the toilet / when / I / see / the actress

6 ? / Charles Dickens / used to / be / a writer

**D The words in bold are wrong. Write the correct words.**

1 In Neolithic times, people used to **hunting** for food. _____

2 Samira wasn't used to **be** on a plane and she didn't like it. _____

3 **When** we were leaving the museum, the curator called us. _____

4 I couldn't **got** used to being famous. _____

5 I was walking on the beach **as** I found a fossil. _____

6 Tom **wouldn't** hate history as a boy, but he does now. _____

## Solve it!

**A Find six words to do with film actors and six words to do with museums in the puzzle. Write them below.**

| S | O | P | R | E | S | E | R | V | E | D | E | R | N |
|---|---|---|---|---|---|---|---|---|---|---|---|---|---|
| F | I | B | F | Z | D | R | A | M | A | R | I | C | E |
| E | N | R | P | E | R | F | O | R | M | A | N | C | E |
| N | T | A | J | A | N | I | G | N | E | U | C | I | X |
| L | E | D | L | R | T | C | U | R | A | T | O | R | H |
| A | R | C | H | A | O | L | O | S | T | O | M | Y | I |
| I | V | E | E | Z | B | H | R | A | S | G | E | P | B |
| R | I | N | K | A | E | J | F | I | N | R | D | O | I |
| B | E | G | T | U | P | R | A | L | E | A | Y | B | T |
| I | W | E | Y | T | O | E | D | M | Y | P | L | A | I |
| A | R | C | H | A | N | L | O | G | Y | H | E | W | O |
| O | R | E | Q | R | U | I | N | S | P | E | F | I | N |
| G | A | F | T | O | T | C | Q | U | O | Y | N | T | E |
| V | A | R | C | H | A | E | O | L | O | G | Y | L | Z |
| I | S | T | A | L | E | N | T | M | I | T | S | E | N |

Film actors

_____

_____

_____

_____

_____

_____

Museums

_____

_____

_____

_____

_____

_____

# 3 Leisure

## Quiz

**How many permanent residents does Antarctica have?**

a 0
b about 10,000
c more than 500,000

FOR YOUR SAFETY
DO NOT STAND ON
OUTER BENCHES

These people are among a group of those adventurous travellers who enjoy spending their leisure time in unusual destinations. People have been visiting Antarctica since the 1950s, favouring the towering icebergs and snowy landscapes of this icy continent to a more conventional holiday by the sea. Trips to Antarctica include visits to research stations and wildlife sites as well as participation in outdoor activities such as kayaking, mountaineering and even scuba-diving in freezing cold waters.

Discussion

In your opinion, is it better for young people's free time to be organised or is it better for them to be free to do what they want?

## Reading

Read the blog entries about leisure activities. Where did/will the events mentioned take place?

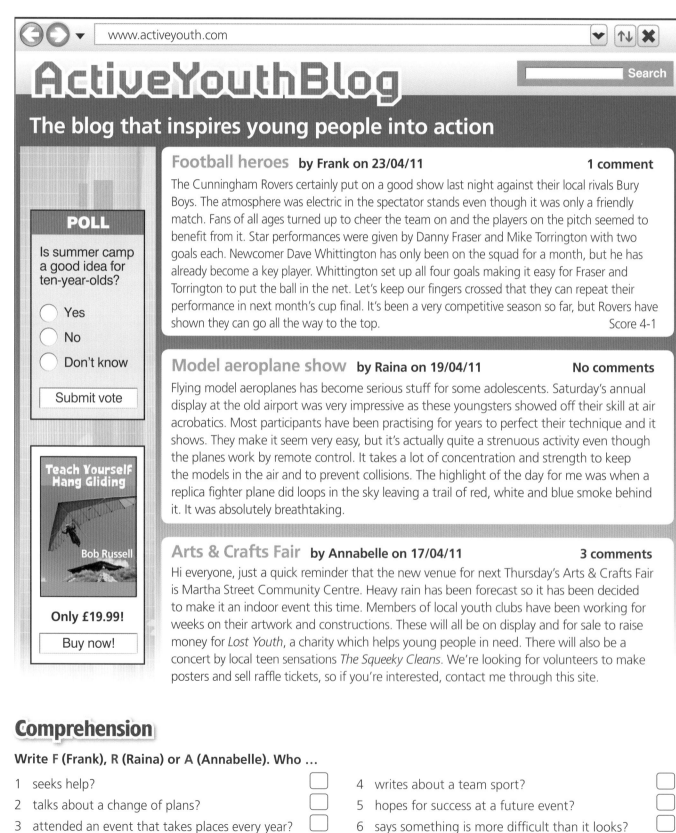

**ActiveYouthBlog**

Search

## The blog that inspires young people into action

**POLL**

Is summer camp a good idea for ten-year-olds?

- ○ Yes
- ○ No
- ○ Don't know

Submit vote

Teach Yourself Hang Gliding

Bob Russell

Only £19.99!

Buy now!

### Football heroes   by Frank on 23/04/11          1 comment

The Cunningham Rovers certainly put on a good show last night against their local rivals Bury Boys. The atmosphere was electric in the spectator stands even though it was only a friendly match. Fans of all ages turned up to cheer the team on and the players on the pitch seemed to benefit from it. Star performances were given by Danny Fraser and Mike Torrington with two goals each. Newcomer Dave Whittington has only been on the squad for a month, but he has already become a key player. Whittington set up all four goals making it easy for Fraser and Torrington to put the ball in the net. Let's keep our fingers crossed that they can repeat their performance in next month's cup final. It's been a very competitive season so far, but Rovers have shown they can go all the way to the top.                                        Score 4-1

### Model aeroplane show   by Raina on 19/04/11          No comments

Flying model aeroplanes has become serious stuff for some adolescents. Saturday's annual display at the old airport was very impressive as these youngsters showed off their skill at air acrobatics. Most participants have been practising for years to perfect their technique and it shows. They make it seem very easy, but it's actually quite a strenuous activity even though the planes work by remote control. It takes a lot of concentration and strength to keep the models in the air and to prevent collisions. The highlight of the day for me was when a replica fighter plane did loops in the sky leaving a trail of red, white and blue smoke behind it. It was absolutely breathtaking.

### Arts & Crafts Fair   by Annabelle on 17/04/11          3 comments

Hi everyone, just a quick reminder that the new venue for next Thursday's Arts & Crafts Fair is Martha Street Community Centre. Heavy rain has been forecast so it has been decided to make it an indoor event this time. Members of local youth clubs have been working for weeks on their artwork and constructions. These will all be on display and for sale to raise money for *Lost Youth*, a charity which helps young people in need. There will also be a concert by local teen sensations *The Squeeky Cleans*. We're looking for volunteers to make posters and sell raffle tickets, so if you're interested, contact me through this site.

## Comprehension

**Write F (Frank), R (Raina) or A (Annabelle). Who ...**

1  seeks help?                                              ☐
2  talks about a change of plans?                           ☐
3  attended an event that takes places every year?          ☐

4  writes about a team sport?                               ☐
5  hopes for success at a future event?                     ☐
6  says something is more difficult than it looks?          ☐

# Vocabulary

**Find the words in the text and circle the correct meaning, a or b.**

1 squad
   a team
   b crew

2 showed off
   a boasted about
   b displayed

3 strenuous
   a determined
   b requiring lots of effort

4 constructions
   a buildings
   b models

5 raise
   a lift
   b collect

6 sensations
   a feelings
   b people causing excitement

# Grammar

## Present Perfect Simple and Present Perfect Continuous

We use the Present Perfect Simple to talk about actions or states that started in the past and are still happening or exist; to talk about actions that have just finished; to talk about actions or states we experienced in the past; and to talk about actions that happened in the past but have results that affect the present. The Present Perfect Simple can also tell us how much or how many times an action has happened.

*Sam has been on the team for years.*
*Amani has won the competition four times.*
*Claire has missed the bus and will be late for the show.*

We use the Present Perfect Continuous to talk about things that started in the past and continue to the present; to talk about recent actions that have happened repeatedly; to say how long something has been happening from the past up to now; and to talk about an action that happened and may have finished in the past, but that has visible results in the present.

*We have been going to the gym every day.*
*Gayle has been writing poetry since she was 16.*
*The kids are tired because they've been playing all day.*

**Note:** We can use the passive in the Present Perfect Simple, but not in the Present Perfect Continuous.
*Brian has been chosen to run the youth club.*

**A** Look back at the text. Underline the verbs in the Present Perfect Simple and circle the verbs in the Present Perfect Continuous. How many are there of each? Which two verbs are in the passive?

**B** Complete the sentences with the Present Perfect Simple (active or passive) or the Present Perfect Continuous of the verbs in brackets.

1 They _____ (play) darts for hours.

2 Oh no! I _____ (not bring) my skates!

3 How many tourists _____ (arrive)?

4 I'm tired because I _____ (read) all day.

5 How long _____ (the coach/talk) to the reporter?

6 The club _____ (give) £30,000 by the local council.

# Word formation

**A Complete the table.**

| Verb | Noun | |
| --- | --- | --- |
| | **Person** | **Thing** |
| spectate | (1) _____ | spectacle |
| perform | performer | (2) _____ |
| (3) _____ | participant | participation |
| train | trainer | (4) _____ |
| support | (5) _____ | support |

**B Circle the correct words.**

1 Sam doesn't support / supporter our football squad.

2 You must train / training hard.

3 Is Robert a good performance / performer?

4 Participation / Participants in the race is free.

5 A spectator / spectacle threw a can onto the pitch.

# Speaking

**Work with a partner and interview each other about your hobbies and pastimes. Use How long, How many times, so far, already, for weeks/months/years and since.**

# Writing

**Write an interview between a reporter for a college magazine and a student. Use the ideas from the Speaking task and ask about these things:**

a a hobby that he/she has done for some time.

b a hobby he/she has recently taken up.

c his/her favourite spectator sport.

**Discussion**

'It is less risky to do extreme sports than it is to do no exercise at all.' Discuss.

## Reading

**Read the article about extreme activities. Which activity was once used to save lives?**

# Go with the flow on the Zambezi

Are you one of those people who just can't sit still? Is the thought of a holiday doing nothing by the sea in your spare time something which you just can't bear? (1) _____

The Zambezi, which is about 3,450 km in length, forms a natural border between Zimbabwe and Zambia and flows down into the Mozambique Channel. (2) _____ The Falls, which was designated a World Heritage Site in 1989, is 1,700 m wide and has a sheer drop of 108 m, so it comes as no surprise that it has become a popular destination for extreme sports enthusiasts.

(3) _____ For those who are truly bold, there's bungee jumping off the Falls, gorge swinging across the river or plunging into Devil's Pool. Activities available along other parts of the Zambezi are white water rafting (which involves a steep hike up a gorge first), flying a microlight plane and river boarding. River boarding, which was originally used as a means of rescue on the river, is an exhilarating way to have fun on your stomach while speeding down the rapids.

If you don't fancy getting soaked or hanging in mid-air, however, you can stay on dry land and participate in activities that bring you into contact with the unique African wildlife. For adventurous types, there are 7-day cycling trips from Nyika Plateau, elephant-back trails or lion encounters to choose from. You will be accompanied by trained guides who will let you in on the secrets of the region. (4) _____ During full moons at the Victoria Falls, an amazing rainbow is visible, created by the moonlight reflected on the waterfall's spray.

(5) _____ The Zambezi is head and shoulders above other destinations and its natural beauty can't help but make a lasting impression on you.

**Guess what!**

*Victoria Falls is known locally as Mosi-oa-Tunya. This means 'the smoke that thunders'.*

## Comprehension

**Complete the article with these sentences.**

a If you want to slow the pace down a bit, however, then why not go moonbow gazing?

b Whatever visitors to the area decide to do, they won't be let down.

c A wealth of activities is on offer here.

d Then head for the river Zambezi in Africa.

e The region's stunning natural landscape boasts one of the wonders of the natural world: the Victoria Falls.

# Vocabulary

Find words or phrases in the article which mean the same as the words in bold. The words are in the same order as they appear in the text.

1 Jack is too active and can't **stop moving** even for a minute.

2 We loved **becoming really wet** when we went white water rafting.

3 Lion encounters and elephant-back rides **allow you to get close to** wildlife.

4 I think river boarding is **far better than** canoeing.

5 The view of the mountain will **be something you'll never forget**.

6 I want to **take it easy** this weekend.

# Grammar

## Relative clauses

We use relative clauses to give more information about people, animals, places and things. Relative clauses begin with relative pronouns (who, whom, which, whose and that) or relative adverbs (where, when and why).
*That's the man who injured himself on the ski slopes.*
*I don't understand the reason why we can't go climbing today.*

We use **defining relative clauses** to give essential information about a person, animal, place or thing. We don't use commas. We can use that instead of which or who, and when the relative pronoun or adverb refers to the object of the clause, we can omit it.
*The guide who/that was in charge took too many risks.*
*The activity (which) I enjoyed most was the river slide.*

We use **non-defining relative clauses** to give extra, non-essential information about a person, animal, place or thing. We use commas to separate the clause from the rest of the sentence. We can't use that instead of who or which, and we can never omit the relative pronoun or adverb.

*The lion cubs, which were two weeks old, were very cute.*

Note: A relative adverb can be used instead of a relative pronoun and a preposition. When can replace in/on which; where can replace in/at which; and why can replace for which.
*This is the city where you can go souvenir hunting.*
*This is the city in which you can go souvenir hunting.*

**A Look at the relative clauses highlighted in the article and answer the questions.**

1 Which is defining and which is non-defining?

2 In which can we replace the relative pronoun with *that*?

3 In which can we omit the relative pronoun? Why?

4 How many other examples of each type of clause can you find?

**B The words in bold are wrong. Write the correct words.**

1 The ball, **who** is red, is on the grass. _____

2 That's the pool **on** which Jane swims. _____

3 That's the guide **which** talks are boring. _____

4 Here is the café **whose** I come every day. _____

5 That lady, **that** won the race, is happy. _____

6 Friday is the day on **when** he trains. _____

# Vocabulary

Circle the correct words.

1 Pete's so bold / timid. He loves extreme sports.

2 Bungee jumping is a safe / risky sport.

3 The film was so exhilarating / dull, I fell asleep.

4 River slides have become very unique / common.

5 You must be very reckless / cautious on the rapids.

6 The guide is great. He's very amateurish / professional.

# Listening

🎧 Listen and number the pictures in the correct order.

## Phrasal Verbs

**Complete the sentences with these words.**

| down | in on | off | off with | on to | out of |
|------|-------|-----|----------|-------|--------|

1 They let us _____ a warning for fighting on the school trip.

2 You let the team _____ when you left suddenly.

3 The trainer let us _____ some of the secrets of mountain climbing.

4 When we arrived at camp after the hike we let _____ some fireworks.

5 Don't let _____ Dad that we're going bungee jumping.

6 The guide didn't let us _____ the car during the safari.

## Vocabulary

**A  Match.**

1  I'll give it a miss.
2  It's a plan.
3  You're not keen on it.
4  I'm at a loose end.
5  I can't believe my ears.
6  Please give me some moral support.

a  We'll meet tomorrow evening.
b  I've got nothing to do.
c  It can't be true.
d  I need some encouragement.
e  I won't attend.
f  You don't fancy it.

**B  Look at the photo of the woman on the right. Which of the sentences from A do you think she could be saying?**

## Listening skills

**A  🎧 Listen to Ron and Sharren talking and decide who does the following. Write R (Ron) or S (Sharren).**

**Who**

1  invites the other person to watch a handball match?
2  describes the atmosphere at the sports centre?
3  says he/she has taken up a new pastime?
4  sounds very surprised?

**B  🎧 Now listen to the dialogue again and change the words in bold to make the sentences true.**

1  Sharren invites Ron to watch the men's team **training**.  _____
2  Ron asks if it's **the cup final** tonight.  _____
3  Ron has taken up **a team sport**.  _____
4  Sharren says Ron used to be the team's **best player**.  _____

## Listening task

🎧 **Listen to Darren and Andrew talking about what to do at the weekend. Decide whether each statement is right (A) or wrong (B).**

|  |  | A | B |
|---|---|---|---|
| 1 | Andrew hasn't decided what to do at the weekend. | ☐ | ☐ |
| 2 | Andrew rejects Darren's offer to watch him play. | ☐ | ☐ |
| 3 | Darren's mum has invited Andrew to lunch on Friday. | ☐ | ☐ |
| 4 | Darren suggests they see a film on Saturday. | ☐ | ☐ |
| 5 | Darren and Andrew arrange to see the film at 6 o'clock. | ☐ | ☐ |
| 6 | Andrew has already been on the London Eye. | ☐ | ☐ |

## Speculating

I'm not sure, but maybe/perhaps he/she is/they're …

He/She is/They're probably …

He/She/They might/may/could/must …

I imagine/guess he/she is/they're …

It's possible/likely that he/she is/they're …

You have to be very fit/adventurous/bold/determined to do …

It takes a lot of concentration/skill/energy/ self-discipline to do …

# Listen Up!

🎧 **Listen to a woman describing a picture and tick (✓) the picture she is talking about. Which expressions from *Express Yourself!* does the speaker use?**

# Speaking skills

**A** Look at the task and the picture in B and put T next to the sentences the son or daughter might say and P next to those the parent might say.

1 You probably have to be a trained pilot. ☐

2 It must be extremely dangerous. ☐

3 It'll be an amazing experience. ☐

4 It's likely that there'll be an accident. ☐

5 I'm sure the trainers are always very cautious. ☐

6 I guess we'll be trained before we do it. ☐

**B** Work with a partner and role-play a discussion between a parent and a teenager. The teenager will try to persuade the parent to let him/her take up the activity in the picture (microlighting). The parent should present reasons why he/she won't give permission.

# Speaking tasks

**A** Look at the task in B. What two things must each partner do?

**B** Work with a partner and take it in turns to describe what's happening in these pictures and say how you think the people are feeling. Student A should talk about picture 1 and Student B should talk about picture 2.

**C** Now talk to your partner about the activity in B that appeals to you most and say what kind of skills you need to have to do it.

## Editing

> When you have finished a piece of writing, you should always spend some time reviewing it and checking for mistakes. Look for errors with grammar, word order, punctuation, spelling and vocabulary.

**Tick (✓) the sentences which are correct and correct the ones that are wrong.**

1  The youth club has been recently preparing an art exhibition. ☐

2  We haven't gone hiking since last autumn. ☐

3  The park where Janice works is closed this week. ☐

4  The Niagara Falls which is in Canada is very popular with tourists. ☐

5  I've done so many activites since I arrived at the camp. ☐

6  Fewer children have come to the camp these year. ☐

7  We've been going for swimming every day. ☐

8  This is the most exiting safari we've been on. ☐

# Writing task

**A  Read this writing task and make a list of the kind of activities on offer at a summer camp. What adjectives could you use to describe them?**

*This is part of an email you receive from a friend.*

> I can't wait to hear about what you've been doing at the summer camp this year. What activities have you been taking part in? Which ones are your favourites? Send me an email soon.

*Now write an email answering your friend's questions.*

**B  Read the model email and find and correct eight mistakes.**

 *model composition*

⊖ ⊖ ⊖                                    **Email**

📧 New      📩 Reply      📨 Forward      🖨 Print      🗑 Delete

Hi Dunya,

Thanks for your email. At last I've got half an hour to write and tell you about the camp! I've been here for two weaks now and I've taken part in lots of activities. The weather hasn't really been good enough for things like canoeing and basketball, but there are lots of other things to do, so it doesn't matter. Let me tell you about my two favourite activities.

The first one is the drama club. We've been preparing for a performance who we'll give next week. We've written the script and making the costumes. I play a doctor! It's taken a lot of work, but hopefully it'll be worth it.

Another activity that I've enjoyed really is trekking. We do this early in the morning, rain or shine. Its never too cold or wet to go trekking! Sometimes I feel too tired to keep going, but I've seen so much wildlife that I wouldn't have seen otherwise. I've become quiet fit too.

It's been so far a wonderful summer. It's just a shame there isn't enough time to do everything! Shall I send you tickets for the performance!

See you soon.

Love,

Vanessa

# Analyse it!

**Tick (✓) the things that Vanessa does in her email.**

1 greets the reader ☐
2 gives the reason for writing ☐
3 gives details about two activities ☐
4 describes the conditions in the camp ☐
5 complains about the other kids ☐
6 invites the reader to a show ☐

# Writing plan

**Complete the plan for the model email with these points.**

> a  briefly talk about the camp in general
> b  describe another activity
> c  describe one of the favourite activities
> d  give the reader a reason to reply
> e  introduce the main point of the email
> f  make a general statement to close the email

| | |
|---|---|
| Greeting | Hi Dunya, |
| Paragraph 1 | Thank reader for previous email; _____ and _____ |
| Paragraph 2 | _____ and give details about what it involves |
| Paragraph 3 | _____ and give details about what it involves |
| Paragraph 4 | _____ and _____ |
| Closing sentence | See you soon. |
| Signing off | Love, Vanessa |

# Grammar

## Too and enough

We use too to show that there is more of something than we need or want. It is followed by an adjective or a determiner.
*I'm too scared to go white water rafting.*
*This adventure holiday costs too much money.*

We use enough to show that there is as much of something as we need. It comes after an adjective.
*Windsurfing is challenging enough for the boldest people.*

We can also use (not) enough before uncountable nouns and plural countable nouns. When it is affirmative it shows that we have got as much of something that we need, but when it is negative it shows that there is less of something than we need.
*There's enough room for both of us in the tent.*
*The centre didn't have enough safety helmets for everyone.*

**Complete the sentences with too or enough.**

1  Is Jack old _____ to go mountain climbing?
2  Don't worry, there are _____ life jackets for the whole team.
3  This activity is _____ dangerous for people who can't swim.
4  The children at the camp make _____ much noise at bedtime.
5  We haven't got _____ time to train for the match.
6  It's not _____ late to go to the park.

# Writing task

*This is part of an email you receive from a friend.*

> I can't believe that you have gone on an adventure holiday in Africa. What have you been doing there? Have you tried any new sports?

*Now write an email answering your friend's questions.*

## Write right!

**Use these steps to help you write your email.**

**Step 1**  Underline the questions in the Writing task that you must answer in your email.

**Step 2**  Make a list of possible sports and activities you could do on this type of holiday.

**Step 3**  Research and make notes about any activities that you don't know enough about.

**Step 4**  Make a plan for your email. Use the plan on the left to help you.

**Step 5**  Use your notes, your plan and the useful language above to write your email.

**Step 6**  Edit your email when you have finished to check for mistakes.

## Discussion

'Sports are the best way to spend your free time.' How far is this true for:
a  players?
b  spectators?

# 4 Town and Country

This rooftop garden sits upon the city hall of Chicago, Illinois. An increasing trend in cities worldwide is to plant trees and other types of greenery on the tops of skyscrapers, in an effort to reduce air pollution and city temperatures. These green spaces can also provide fresh fruits and vegetables and can be seen not only on rooftops but on the walls of buildings as well. In 2009, the City of Dubai decided that all new buildings there should have roof gardens.

## Lesson 1

**Discussion**

'Living in the countryside is really boring.' Discuss.

## Reading

Read the interview with a young person to find out who had problems living in the countryside.

# Country Life

*We interviewed 16-year-old Ada Carrington, who lives on a farm in Devon, about life in the sticks.*

**Interviewer:** Ada, your surroundings are picturesque, but is life in a remote location really suitable for someone your age?

**Ada:** It's got its drawbacks, but I think I'm privileged to have grown up here.

**Interviewer:** In what ways?

**Ada:** Well, for a start the pace of life is much slower. The peace and quiet has helped me progress with my schoolwork because there are fewer distractions.

**Interviewer:** Does that mean there aren't enough leisure facilities for someone your age?

**Ada:** The facilities are pretty poor. The nearest shops, sports centre and theatre are 15 kilometres away. As you can imagine, there isn't a regular bus service so I have to rely on my parents or my brother Paul to give me a lift to town and back.

**Interviewer:** That sounds tough, but I suppose you are used to it if you have always lived here.

**Ada:** That's right. Last year there was a boy in my class, Zak, who had been living in London before his family moved here. He'd been brought up in the hustle and bustle of the capital so he was used to everything on a large scale. It really hit him hard that there are fewer choices here.

**Interviewer:** Don't you ever get lonely living so far out of the way?

**Ada:** Not really; I see my best friends every day. Mum always says it's better to have personal contact with fewer people than to be surrounded by hundreds of strangers.

**Interviewer:** Wise words. But what happens in emergencies? Are there sufficient emergency services nearby?

**Ada:** Not within walking distance, but our district has several well-organised hospitals. Last summer, for example, Paul had been working in the orchards and was climbing down from a tree when he fell and broke his arm. Luckily, I was nearby because I had been picking apples too, so I heard him scream. Mum and Dad were out, so I phoned for an ambulance. It only took twenty minutes to get here because the roads are so quiet and Paul saw a doctor immediately because the hospital wasn't busy.

**Interviewer:** That is impressive. So what does the future hold for you?

**Ada:** I hope to go to Edinburgh University in two years' time to study law.

**Interviewer:** So you'll be swapping rural life for the bright lights!

**Ada:** That's right. Who knows, I might even prefer an urban environment!

## Comprehension

**Answer the questions.**

1 What has having few distractions allowed Ada to do?
2 Why does Ada need people to drive her around?
3 Why does Ada mention Zak?
4 How did Paul get to hospital when he had an accident?
5 What does Ada plan to do in the future?

## Vocabulary

**Circle the correct words.**

1 This city isn't wise / picturesque, but it's a nice place to live.
2 Rural life's biggest drawback / distraction is the lack of facilities.
3 Pat feels really privileged / sufficient to be living close to nature.
4 Everything in cities is on a large scale / distance.
5 I love the bright / urban lights of the city.

# Grammar

## Past Perfect Continuous

We use the Past Perfect Continuous to talk about:

a  an action that was in progress for some time in the past before another past action interrupted it.
*They had been driving for hours when they finally reached the town.*

b  an action that was in progress in the past which affected a later action or state.
*It had been snowing all night so the mountains were completely white.*

We make the Past Perfect Continuous with had been and the verb + –ing.

### Affirmative

I'd (I had) been walking.

### Negative

I hadn't (had not) been walking.

### Question

Had you been walking ...?

### Short answers

Yes, I had./No, I hadn't.

### Time expressions

| | |
|---|---|
| all day/night/week | since 2 o'clock/yesterday |
| for years/a long time | at the time |

## A  Choose the correct answers.

1  'Had you been living in the cottage for long?'
'No, _____ .'
   a  hadn't we
   b  we hadn't been
   c  we hadn't

2  She'd _____ for hours outside the theatre when he finally turned up.
   a  waited
   b  been waiting
   c  had been

3  Had Derek been _____ all morning?
   a  shopping
   b  shopped
   c  to shop

4  They _____ been digging the garden when I arrived.
   a  're
   b  'd
   c  've

5  _____ when they saw the brown bear.
   a  They have not eaten
   b  They hadn't been eating
   c  Had they been eating

6  She had been picking strawberries _____ morning.
   a  for
   b  at
   c  all

## B  Write sentences with the Past Perfect Continuous.

1  the villagers / complain / about the poor facilities / for years

2  the mayor / give a speech / when the lights went out

3  ? / the farmer / work / since 5 am

4  they / not play / for long / when we arrived

5  the train driver / not pay attention / at the time of the accident

6  the dog was wet because / it / swim / in the river

## Collocations

Complete the sentences with these phrases.

| |
|---|
| doom and gloom    hustle and bustle |
| ins and outs    peace and quiet |
| pros and cons    tooth and nail |

1  The residents have been fighting _____ for better medical facilities.

2  I'm going to my house in the countryside for some _____ this weekend.

3  Some people love the _____ of busy cities.

4  How does this scheme work? I don't understand the _____ of it.

5  Don't moan all the time! Living in the country is not all _____!

6  What are the _____ of living in a quiet town like Whitby?

## Speaking

Ask and answer these questions with your partner.

1  What is the area you live in like?

2  What kind of facilities do you use regularly?

3  Are there any facilities missing from your area?

4  Is it better for someone your age to live in a city or in a village? Why?

5  Where would you choose to live if you could go anywhere? Why?

## Writing

Write two paragraphs about the place where you live and the place where you would like to live. Answer the questions from the Speaking task.

**Discussion**

Discuss the advantages and disadvantages of opening a zoo in a city.

## Reading

Read the article to find out what's unusual about the neighbours it mentions.

# Wildlife in the city

The district of Overton Park in Memphis, Tennessee, is a residential area, but the residents don't live in an ordinary suburb. Their neighbours are a bit wilder than most people's, but they don't seem to mind. This is because the park, which was turned into a zoological and botanical garden in 1906, is now home to 3,500 animals from 500 different species.

Visitors to the zoo can see creatures such as polar bears, seals, komodo dragons and bald eagles. Bald eagles are native to this area as they naturally migrate here in winter, but aren't the others a bit far from home? They certainly are, but they reside in environments which are as close to the animals' natural habitats as zookeepers can make them.

There are undoubtedly drawbacks to keeping animals in captivity, but it cannot be denied that zoos play an important part in saving endangered species. Researchers at zoos are able to learn more about certain species that would be impossible to study in the wild. Furthermore, animals that had once been at risk are now protected due to the conservation policies at zoos. It's a sad fact that human activity all over the world had been causing the destruction or loss of some species' natural habitats long before we realised it. This is why one of the basic roles of zoos today should be to educate the public about how the natural world works and how we affect species and their habitats both positively and negatively. The staff of Memphis Zoo take this part of their job very seriously and realise they are responsible not only for the animals, but also for instructing visitors and the local community about nature's delicate balance.

We don't just live alongside nature, we are part of it and we must learn to appreciate the value and importance of all our neighbours – plant or animal, near or far.

## Comprehension

**Write A if the sentence is correct and B if it is not correct.**

1  There are 3,500 species of animals at Memphis Zoo.

2  You can only see bald eagles in winter at Memphis Zoo.

3  Zoos have some disadvantages.

4  The staff at Memphis Zoo try to educate the public.

5  Some plants and animals are more valuable than others.

**Guess what!**
Adult polar bears can weigh up to 680 kg, but at birth polar bear cubs weigh less than 0.9 kg!

# Vocabulary

**Find words or phrases in the article that have these meanings. The words are in the same order as they appear in the text.**

1 district on the edge of a city _____

2 belonging to a particular area or country _____

3 the place where an animal lives in the wild _____

4 plans of action _____

5 a group of people who live in the same area _____

6 easily damaged _____

# Grammar

## Past Perfect Simple and Past Perfect Continuous

We use the Past Perfect Simple to talk about something that happened before another action in the past; to talk about something that happened before a specific time in the past; and to talk about something that happened in the past and had an effect on a later action.
*The bear had already left when the family returned home.*
*They'd taken the cub back to the woods by ten o'clock.*
*Karen had forgotten her key, so she couldn't get in.*

We use the Past Perfect Continuous to talk about an action that was in progress for some time in the past before another past action interrupted it; and to talk about an action that was in progress in the past which affected a later action or state.
*Jack had been cutting down a tree when he fell over.*
*I'd been gardening for hours so I was exhausted.*

We use both tenses to talk about actions that happened in the past before another past action. We use the Past Perfect Continuous to emphasise how long the first action was in progress or to show that we don't know whether the action was completed or not.
*They had arrived at the park by 10 am.*
*I'd been wandering round the zoo all day, so I was tired.*

**A Complete the text with the Past Perfect Simple or the Past Perfect Continuous of the verbs in brackets.**

Hyderabad in India is one of the world's fastest growing cities. Its population (1) _____ (already reach) more than five million by 2009. It (2) _____ (always be) an important city and it (3) _____ (attract) migrants from all over India for centuries before the population grew out of control.

The Hyderabad Urban Development Authority (4) _____ (look) for opportunities to make the city greener for some time when they came across an old factory. The Lumbini Park was built on the site of the factory and it has brought a breath of fresh air to the city. The residents (5) _____ (not realise) just how essential open space was to the quality of their lives.

**B Look at the phrases highlighted in the text. Say which tense has been used in each case and explain why.**

# Vocabulary

**Match.**

1 adventure playground ☐
2 botanical garden ☐
3 city landscape ☐
4 community centre ☐
5 open country ☐
6 residential area ☐

# Listening

🎧 **Listen to three teenagers talking about where they live. Tick (✓) the facilities found in each person's area.**

|  | Elias | Michael | Shona |
|---|---|---|---|
| café |  |  |  |
| cinema |  |  |  |
| community centre |  |  |  |
| library |  |  |  |
| park |  |  |  |
| sports centre |  |  |  |

## Prepositions

**Complete the sentences with in or on.**

1 Animals often live longer ____ captivity.

2 There are few examples of this species ____ the wild.

3 Reports say there's a moose ____ the loose in our town.

4 I've just bought a new house ____ the outskirts of town.

5 Living ____ the suburbs can be boring.

6 People shouldn't have to live ____ the streets these days.

## Vocabulary

**Match.**

1  I'm shocked by the living
2  It's normally poor families that live in inner
3  The number of homeless people has reached
4  There's the doctor who runs the country
5  I've just read a shocking
6  Some people are attracted by the bright

a  record levels this decade.
b  practice.
c  lights of big cities.
d  report about health care.
e  cities.
f  conditions in this city.

## Listening skills

**A  Decide which sentence, a or b, is closest in meaning to the sentences in 1 and 2.**

1  I don't know why anyone would want to live in an inner city.
   a  I don't understand why people live in a city centre.
   b  I don't know anyone who lives in an inner city.

2  Damian now knows that living in remote locations has its drawbacks.
   a  Damian realises rural life has got disadvantages.
   b  Damian always knew that living in remote locations isn't easy.

**B  🎧 Listen to these speakers. How do they express the meaning of the words and phrases in bold in these sentences?**

1  The boy says **there aren't enough things to do** in his village for **people his age**.
2  The girl really likes the **lack of noise** in the countryside.
3  The woman **was surprised** when she saw a fox **eating** in her garden.
4  The man says that in his town **there are more people out of work than ever before**.

## Listening task

🎧 **You will hear a preview of tonight's television programmes. For each question, put a tick (✓) in the correct box.**

1  Tonight's episode of *Grass Roots* is
   a  the last in the series.  ☐
   b  on at seven o'clock.  ☐
   c  set in a big city.  ☐

2  *Into the Fire*
   a  is filmed in a small country practice.  ☐
   b  shows a manager in a busy hospital.  ☐
   c  shows people who change their workplace.  ☐

3  The soap opera mentioned
   a  is watched by many viewers.  ☐
   b  will be replaced by a documentary tonight.  ☐
   c  shows how glamorous the city is.  ☐

4  Rory Jordan died
   a  because a brown bear bit him.  ☐
   b  due to illness.  ☐
   c  while making an hour-long documentary.  ☐

5  The news
   a  will be on later than usual.  ☐
   b  is shown at nine o'clock.  ☐
   c  follows the weather forecast.  ☐

6  The news report mentioned
   a  is all about crime.  ☐
   b  will be about careers in inner cities.  ☐
   c  deals with a national problem.  ☐

# express yourself!

## Justifying choices

More people would benefit from …

… only appeals to young/old/sporty/etc people.

… would be more useful/better for the whole community.

… is more necessary/important than …

… is missing in this city/town/village.

I think it's a good idea to … because …

There's a real need for …

I don't see the point in + -ing … / … is pointless.

It's a waste of money to + infinitive … / … is a waste of money.

# Listen Up!

**A** 🎧 **Listen to Simon and Ella doing the Speaking task below and write S (Simon), E (Ella) or B (Both) to show who does these things.**

*A friend of yours is taking a group of teenagers from the countryside to the city for an evening. Look at the pictures and work with a partner to discuss the kinds of places he could take them to and decide which two are the most entertaining.*

Who

1   use(s) appropriate language?

2   listen(s) to the other person?

3   develop(s) his/her answers?

4   make(s) the most appropriate choices for the situation?

**B   Do they complete the task properly?**

# Speaking skills

**A   Read the task in B and tick (✓) the factors you might have to think about when reaching a decision.**

1   age of people concerned

2   your own interests

3   cost of event/facilities

4   special needs people might have

5   the aim of the people concerned

**B   Work with a partner and role play a dialogue between the mayor and his/her 14-year-old son/daughter about what facilities their district needs. Use these words and the phrases in *Express Yourself!* to help you.**

| | |
|---|---|
| adventure playground | public library |
| bicycle lanes | shopping mall |
| community centre | sports centre |
| country park | theatre |

# Speaking tasks

**A   Look at the Speaking task in B below and answer these questions.**

1   What kind of facilities will you discuss?

2   Who are these facilities for?

3   How many facilities will you decide on at the end?

4   Do you have to reach an agreement with your partner?

**B   The local community in the village where you live has been given money to improve facilities for residents. Look at the pictures and work with a partner to talk about the kind of facilities that could be provided, and decide which two are most important for all villagers.**

## Narrative tenses

Narrative tenses are used when telling a story in the past. The most common ones are the Past Simple, the Past Continuous, the Past Perfect Simple and the Past Perfect Continuous. We do not use present tenses at all unless the story we are writing includes direct speech with speech marks.

**A  Complete the table with the correct tense.**

Past Continuous    Past Perfect Simple    Past Perfect Continuous    Past Simple

| _____ | _____ |
|---|---|
| • talks about a completed action in the past<br>• takes action of the story further<br>• talks about a series of actions that happened one after the other in the past | • talks about an action that happened before the time of the narrative or before another past action<br>• talks about a past action that interrupts another action in the past |
| _____ | _____ |
| • talks about an action in progress in the past when another action interrupted it<br>• describes background details in the story | • talks about an action that was in progress for some time in the past and had an effect on a later event<br>• talks about an action that was in progress for some time in the past when it was interrupted by another past action |

**B  Which tenses are used in the following sentences? Why?**

1  *She slammed the door, ran to the wardrobe and hid inside it.*

2  *They had been walking for hours and Jo was losing her patience.*

3  *I was waiting at the bus stop when I first saw Sally.*

4  *Daisy stopped. The doll wasn't where she had left it.*

## Writing task

**Read the story written by a student who has done the following writing task. Which tenses are the highlighted verbs in? Why have these tenses been used?**

**Write a story which begins with this sentence:**
*I knew something was wrong as soon as I went into the garden.*

# Bear for lunch

After lunch I decided to go out. I knew something was wrong as soon as I went into the garden. My cat, Jody, was shaking with fear on the doorstep. I was bending down to comfort her when I realised why she was so afraid.
A visitor had wandered in from the woods.

Recovering quickly, I picked up Jody, rushed inside and locked the kitchen door.

'Mum, there's a bear in the garden!' I yelled.

'It'll only be the neighbour's dog again,' Mum said, trying to calm me down.

'But look …'.

Just then the rubbish bin crashed to the ground so we ran to the window. While we had been talking, the bear had eaten the contents of our bin. Mum was terrified.

Suddenly, I had an idea. I remembered that Dad had been reading an article on wild animals in residential areas. Maybe that would tell us what to do. Luckily, it had the phone number of the local Wild Animal Rescue Service.

The people from the rescue service acted immediately and soon the bear was back in the wild. It was a scary experience, but one I'll never forget.

# Analyse it!

**Answer these questions.**

1 What serious mistake has the writer of the story made? Correct it.
2 Which verbs, adjectives and adverbs does the writer use to create suspense and keep the reader interested?
3 What happens at the beginning, the middle and the end of the story?
4 Is the story written with informal, semi-formal or formal language?

# Writing plan

**Write a number from 1 to 5 in the boxes to show the order in which these things are mentioned in the story.**

a Describe an event that creates suspense in the story. ☐
b Set the scene for the story. ☐
c Say how you managed to deal with the situation. ☐
d Say what happened in the end and how the event affected you. ☐
e Say what you did as soon as you realised something was wrong. ☐

# Grammar

## Articles

We use the indefinite articles a/an with singular countable nouns when we mention them for the first time; when speaking generally; and with nouns which refer to professions, nationalities or religions.
*Look! There's a bear at the window.*          *Gerald is an editor.*

We don't use a/an with plural countable nouns or uncountable nouns; with adjectives which aren't followed by a noun; and with the names of meals unless they are preceded by an adjective.
*Cities have usually got good facilities.*          *What's for dinner?*

We use the definite article the with singular and plural countable and uncountable nouns; to talk about something specific when we mention it a second time; before unique nouns, names of hotels, cinemas, theatres and musical instruments; before superlatives and nationalities; and with the names of natural features.
*This is the village I was telling you about.*
*Our school is the largest in the district.*

We don't use the with proper nouns, the names of sports and games, languages and subjects of study; or with the names of most countries and cities or the names of non-specific facilities.
*She's learning Chinese at college.*          *We often play rugby.*

**Complete the sentences with a, an, the or -.**

1 Let's go for _____ walk round the square.
2 Is that _____ new hotel you told me about?
3 There's a boy from _____ Muscat in my class.
4 There isn't _____ college in our town.
5 Pizza? That's _____ unusual breakfast.
6 There's a play on at _____ Royal Theatre tonight.
7 *Greasy Frank's* is _____ worst restaurant in the city.
8 I think that _____ rural areas are becoming less populated.

# Writing task

*Write a story that begins with this sentence:*
It was the strangest place I had ever been to in my life.

## Write right!

**Use these steps to help you write your story.**

**Step 1**  Underline the key words in the sentence you must use to begin.
**Step 2**  Think of a good idea for the story and decide what the narrator saw. Think about what happens next and how the story will develop. Then think about how the story might end.
**Step 3**  Make a plan and decide how you will organise the events. Use the plan above to help you.
**Step 4**  Use your notes, your plan and the useful language above to write your story. Make sure that you use language and devices which make the story exciting.
**Step 5**  Read your story carefully when you have finished. Check that you have used narrative tenses and that the first sentence fits in the rest of the story.

Discuss the pros and cons of living in a city and the countryside.

# Review 2

## Vocabulary

**A** Match.

| | | | |
|---|---|---|---|
| 1 | lasting | a | area |
| 2 | residential | b | boarding |
| 3 | star | c | impression |
| 4 | adventure | d | garden |
| 5 | river | e | performance |
| 6 | botanical | f | playground |

**B** Circle the odd one out.

| | | | |
|---|---|---|---|
| 1 | let down | show off | display |
| 2 | spectator | supporter | participant |
| 3 | sensations | drawbacks | disadvantages |
| 4 | outskirts | suburbs | inner cities |
| 5 | reckless | picturesque | risky |

**C** Complete the table.

> adolescent   community centre   cup final
> display   fair   orchard   researcher   trainer   venue

| Events | People | Places |
|---|---|---|
| _____ | _____ | _____ |
| _____ | _____ | _____ |
| _____ | _____ | _____ |

**D** Complete the sentences with these words.

> bring   let   native   raise   slow
> soaked   strenuous   urban

1 Let's _____ the pace down a bit.
2 Meetings can _____ residents into contact with each other.
3 A professional trekker _____ me in on a few secrets trails.
4 Moonbow gazing isn't a _____ activity.
5 I prefer _____ life to the countryside.
6 How much money did you _____?
7 We got absolutely _____ when we went horse riding in the rain.
8 What kind of wildlife is _____ to this region?

## Grammar

**A** Choose the correct answers.

1 She has never _____ a model aeroplane before.
   a   been flying
   b   flown
   c   flew

2 Joe is _____ player I told you about earlier.
   a   the
   b   a
   c   -

3 This is the place _____ I did my first bungee jump.
   a   which
   b   when
   c   where

4 There aren't _____ people for a football team.
   a   enough
   b   too
   c   the

5 They _____ living in the village for a month when the flood happened.
   a   have been
   b   had been
   c   had

6 The adventure playground _____ we go to is free.
   a   what
   b   in which
   c   that

**B** Rewrite the sentences using the words in bold. Use between two and five words.

1 Some activities are too risky for children.   **safe**
   Some activities _____
   for children.

2 There's Jo, the trainer of the squad.   **is**
   Jo, _____ squad's
   trainer, is over there.

3 It took us hours to sail to Hull.   **for**
   We _____ hours by
   the time we reached Hull.

4 I've never heard such a strange story before.   **strangest**
   That's _____ I've
   ever heard.

5 I started writing the blog two years ago.   **been**
   I _____ for two years.

48

**C** Complete the paragraph with the correct form of the Present Perfect Simple, Present Perfect Continuous, Past Perfect Simple or Past Perfect Continuous of the verbs in brackets.

Jake (1) _____ (be) an extreme sports enthusiast for many years now. He (2) _____ (go) on adventure holidays and doing risky activities since he was 14 and is always looking for a challenge. So when some friends asked him to be their guide on a hike in open country, he immediately agreed. Jake (3) _____ (never try) to lead a group before, but he was sure he could manage it. Before they left, Jake told the others what kind of clothing to wear and what things to take with them. They set off early one Saturday morning and headed for the countryside. They (4) _____ (walk) for over two hours when they arrived at some woods. They (5) _____ (just enter) the woods when they saw the most beautiful sight they (6) _____ (ever/see). Some deer were drinking from a lake right in front of them. When they arrived back home, they all agreed the hike (7) _____ (be) tiring, but that they (8) _____ (have) an excellent time.

**Choose the correct answers.**

1 What sport is the underwater activity octopush similar to?
   a rugby
   b baseball
   c hockey

2 How many players are there on an ice hockey team?
   a 5
   b 6
   c 7

3 Which weird event takes place every November in Cumbria, UK?
   a The World's Biggest Liar Competition
   b The World Pea Shooting Championships
   c The Animal Olympics

4 What do the residents of Buñol, Spain, do every August?
   a have a carnival
   b throw tomatoes at each other
   c chase each other through the streets

5 How long did the world's longest aerobics class last?
   a 14 hours
   b 24 hours
   c 40 hours

6 Which sport isn't played on a pitch?
   a cricket
   b football
   c badminton

7 In which country did chess originate?
   a India
   b Scotland
   c Brazil

8 What was unusual about the tennis match between Serena Williams and Rafael Nadal in March 2008?
   a It was played on water.
   b It took place in the middle of the night.
   c No spectators turned up.

**Scoring:** Check your answers and score 2 points for each one that is correct. Then see what your score says about you!

**0-4** You're not a great fan of sport and leisure. You prefer to take it easy and not do very much in your free time and it doesn't matter to you how other people spend theirs. Or maybe you are just extremely busy and don't have enough time to spend on leisure activities.

**5-10** You like fun and games, but there are more important things in your life. You like to find out about what's happening in the world of sport, but you don't let this distract you from your schoolwork. You have more important goals in your life.

**11-16** You are a real leisure enthusiast. You must find out the latest scores in your favourite sports and you always read about what's happening in the world of sport. You also like the strange side of leisure and would probably like to take part in extreme sports.

1c 2c 3a 4b 5b 6c 7a 8a

# 5 Journeys

This ship, which now sits at the bottom of the Atlantic Ocean, is the famous *Titanic*. The *Titanic* was a passenger liner that sank after hitting an iceberg in April 1912. It was four days into its maiden voyage from Southampton, England, to New York, USA, when the tragic accident occurred. It was the largest vessel of its kind when it was constructed and it was believed to be unsinkable.

Discussion

'Travellers to foreign countries learn about the cultures of the local people.' Discuss.

# Reading

**Read the book reviews and say which two books are most helpful for people who are planning a journey.**

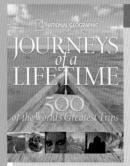

## A Journeys of a Lifetime
*500 of the world's greatest trips*

This 400-page guide features breathtaking photography and has been put together by several of National Geographic's best travel writers. It provides useful information for travellers who enjoy a challenge and who aren't afraid to travel to remote corners of the globe. *Journeys of a Lifetime* is a must for anyone who will be heading off on a voyage of discovery in the near future as it covers all continents and gives advice on travelling by all possible means of transport. There are also plenty of ingenious ideas to make sure your trip will be, without doubt, the journey of a lifetime.

## B The 100 best worldwide vacations to enrich your life
*by Pam Grout*

If you've decided that you're going to do more than just relax on your next holiday, then this book is for you. Pam Grout believes travel should be much more than leisure and encourages travellers to spend their time constructively or in aid of a worthy cause. She presents 100 ideas for activity holidays of all descriptions from learning a skill such as cooking and painting to helping to rebuild communities. The book provides invaluable travel information for holidays that will broaden your horizons.

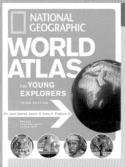

## C National Geographic World Atlas for Young Explorers
*3rd Edition*

This award-winning publication has been updated to include all the latest facts and figures concerning current world geography to make sure young readers have up-to-date knowledge of our world and its people. The atlas is interactive and is linked to a website where users can take part in activities like viewing a reconstruction of the *Titanic* and playing games that instruct them about the nature of tornados. The atlas will not only educate but also stimulate our young explorers without calling for them to leave the safety of their bedrooms. Parents and children alike will love it.

## D In Motion
*The African-American Migration Experience by Howard Dodson and Sylviane A Dioue*

*In Motion* takes readers on a fascinating journey. It traces the roots of the 35 million Americans of African descent and analyses the phases of both voluntary and enforced migration that they experienced. The book shows how the strong cultures and well-organised communities from which the migrants came enabled them to survive these migrations and settle in and develop the Americas. As well as taking a good look at the past, the book also shows the effects these migrations are going to have on the future.

# Comprehension

**Write A, B, C or D.**

**Which book**

1  encourages people to do something useful? ☐
2  contains the latest information on a subject? ☐
3  has definitely been written by more than two people? ☐
4  is aimed at children? ☐
5  looks at historical voyages? ☐
6  promotes creative holidays? ☐
7  talks about people who didn't return from their journey? ☐
8  includes exceptionally good photography? ☐

# Vocabulary

**Complete the sentences with these words.**

| current descent globe ingenious interactive roots |

1  Family trees help us get to know our _____ .
2  Atlases contain maps of every country on the _____ .
3  They don't have any _____ plans to go on holiday.
4  We were given some _____ ideas on how to travel on a low budget.
5  There are many people of British _____ in Australia.
6  There are two _____ DVDs with this guidebook.

# Grammar

## Future Simple, be going to and Future Continuous

We use the Future Simple to make predictions; to talk about decisions we make now for the future; to make offers, promises or give warnings; to ask someone for help; and to state opinions about the future after think, hope, believe, and be sure.
*Everyone will enjoy the excursion.*
*Will you lend me your guide to Antarctica?*
*Grant's sure the journey won't take more than four hours.*

> **Note:** We use shall with the pronouns I and we in questions when we want to offer or suggest something.
> *Shall I ring the travel agency again?*

We use be going to to talk about future plans and intentions and to predict something when we have proof or information.
*Are you going to fly or take the boat?*
*My train has been delayed so I'm not going to arrive in time for the meeting.*

We use the Future Continuous to talk about things that will be in progress at a specific time in the future.
*This time next week, we'll be crossing the Channel.*

### Time expressions with the Future Continuous

this time next week/month/year
in a few days/years/the near future
during the weekend/summer/winter
soon

**A** Underline verbs which refer to the future in the texts. Which tense or form has been used in each case? Why have they been used?

**B** Circle the correct answers.

1 Look! That coach will crash / is going to crash into a lorry.

2 I think we will board / are going to board the plane in half an hour.

3 Will Katrina be ride / riding her bike at this time tomorrow?

4 The ship won't be leaving / isn't going to leave until the captain arrives.

5 Will we plan / Will we be planning our route during the weekend?

6 Stop the car! Anne will / is going to be sick.

7 This bag is heavy. Will you / Are you going to carry it for me, please?

8 Shall / Will I book the tickets for you?

# Word formation

**A** Write en as a prefix or a suffix to make these words into verbs. Which one includes en as a prefix *and* a suffix?

1 _____ able _____       5 _____ rich _____
2 _____ broad _____      6 _____ sharp _____
3 _____ force _____      7 _____ short _____
4 _____ light _____      8 _____ sure _____

**B** Complete the paragraph with the correct form of the verbs from A.

At the age of 17, I decided it was time to (1) _____ my horizons and go on a trip of a lifetime. I packed my rucksack and made all the necessary arrangements that would (2) _____ me to travel by train through Europe. Travelling by train in various countries would (3) _____ my life as I would gain experience, see wonderful sights and also (4) _____ my language skills.

Everything was going well until the second week of the trip. I was in Paris waiting on a busy platform when something happened that made me (5) _____ my trip – I broke my arm. I was zipping up my rucksack when I was pushed onto the track by the man who was standing next to me. The man denied that he had done it, but a woman had seen what had happened and she (6) _____ the police officers when they arrived.

In the end, I was pleased that the police had been there to (7) _____ the law, and I thanked the woman who gave evidence to (8) _____ that the man was charged with the crime, but I was still sad because my trip was over.

# Speaking

Work with a partner. Take it in turns to ask and answer questions about a journey you each want to go on with your family in the future. Use these ideas to help you. Make notes about what your partner says.

the destination             activities to do
means of transport          reason for choosing this destination
sights to see

# Writing

Write an interview about someone's plans for a journey. Use the information your partner gave you in the Speaking task.

## Reading

Read the article about explorers Borge Ousland and Thomas Ulrich. What did Ousland do completely on his own?

### Discussion

'Remote places are the best places on Earth.' Discuss why the following people may have different opinions about this statement:

a travellers
b locals

# Exploring your limits

For most, it would be an impossible journey. For polar explorers Borge Ousland and Thomas Ulrich, however, the expedition from the North Pole to Cape Flora on Northbrook Island, Russia, was just another challenge. Both are very experienced and have broken several records in past exploits in extreme locations and conditions.

On 1st May 2007, Ousland and Ulrich set off from the North Pole. Their aim was to take the same route that Fridtjof Nansen and Hjalmer Johansen had taken in 1895. The explorers' 85-day odyssey involved 1,400 km of skiing, kayaking and kiting across snow-capped lands and seas of drifting ice. On 24th July they reached Cape Flora, where they spent three weeks waiting to be picked up and taken back to Norway.

Unlike Nansen and Johansen 112 years before them, Ousland and Ulrich had the assistance of communication and navigation equipment to keep them on track. On one
18 occasion, while they were sleeping on an ice floe, their GPS warned them that they were moving in the wrong direction. This prompted them into action and they swore not to stop until they reached land.

It takes a special kind of person to battle on against all odds. By the time such a remarkable journey comes to an end, explorers will have been testing themselves to the limit for weeks. They will have had to endure sub-zero temperatures and long periods of darkness. They will also have proven they have the determination and the will to survive that sets them apart from others.

In this respect, Ousland and Ulrich have shown on many occasions that they are truly exceptional. Ousland in particular has been recognised for his extraordinary skills. In February 2006, the *National Geographic Adventurer* wrote 'Borge Ousland is arguably the most accomplished polar explorer alive.' It's easy to see why this opinion was expressed. One of Ousland's many accomplishments was a solo expedition across Antarctica – a journey previously thought impossible.

For those of us who lead sedentary lives, it can be hard to relate to people like Ousland and Ulrich. However, they teach us an important lesson: we should set goals for ourselves and try our hardest to achieve them.

## Comprehension

### Answer the questions.

1  Where did Ousland and Ulrich's 2007 expedition begin?

2  Why did Ousland and Ulrich spend three weeks at Cape Flora?

3  What does the word 'their' in line 18 refer to?

4  What kind of conditions must polar explorers endure?

5  What does the writer conclude about people like Ousland and Ulrich?

### Guess what!

The coldest temperature ever recorded on Earth was -89.2°C at the Russian Vostok Station in Antarctica on 21st July 1983.

# Vocabulary

**Find phrases in the article which mean the same as the words in bold. The words are in the same order as they appear in the text.**

1 They **were helped by** modern navigation equipment.
2 The navigation equipment helped **to prevent them getting lost**.
3 The pair reached their destination **despite all the difficulties**.
4 They're **pushing themselves as far as possible** on this trip.
5 Many people **are very inactive**.
6 We all have to **give ourselves targets** to work towards.

# Grammar

## Future Perfect Simple

We use the Future Perfect Simple to talk about an action that will have been completed before another action or before a specific time in the future.
*Will the expedition have ended by winter?*

We make the Future Perfect Simple with will have + the past participle of the verb. We use the same form for all persons of the verb.

## Future Perfect Continuous

We use the Future Perfect Continuous to talk about how long an action will have been in progress by a specific time in the future.
*We will have been sailing for three days by the time we arrive.*

We make the Future Perfect Continuous with will have been and the verb + -ing. We use the same form for all persons of the verb.

### Affirmative
I'll have been hiking...

### Negative
I won't have been hiking...

| Question | Short answers |
|---|---|
| Will you have been hiking ...? | Yes, I will./No, I won't. |

## Future Perfect Simple or Future Perfect Continuous?

We use the Future Perfect Simple to emphasise the **result** of a future action and the Future Perfect Continuous to emphasise the **duration** of a future action.
*By the autumn, you'll have travelled 1,000 km.*
*By the autumn, you'll have been travelling for a month.*

### Time expressions with both tenses
before ..., by 2.30, by this afternoon, by Wednesday, by the time ..., by the summer, in a week's time, soon

**Complete the sentences with the Future Perfect Simple or the Future Perfect Continuous of the verbs in brackets.**

1 _____ (they/discover) new islands by 2015?
2 She _____ (tour) the area for a month by this time next week.
3 The trip _____ (not end) by Tuesday.
4 They _____ (build) this bridge for years by the time it's finished.
5 We _____ (sail) for five weeks by the end of the cruise.
6 The birds _____ (migrate) by October.

# Vocabulary

**Circle the odd one out.**

| 1 | accomplishment | capability | achievement |
|---|---|---|---|
| 2 | persistence | determination | limitation |
| 3 | endure | support | tolerate |
| 4 | battle | torture | struggle |
| 5 | drifting | stable | floating |

# Listening

🎧 **Listen to these people talking about expeditions and complete the table.**

|  | Journey | Means of transport | Time taken |
|---|---|---|---|
| **Bleakney** | (1) _____ to Argentina | (2) _____ | (3) _____ |
| **Bancroft & Arnesen** | Across (4) _____ | (5) _____ | (6) _____ |
| **Perham** | around (7) _____ | (8) _____ | (9) _____ |

## Phrasal Verbs

**Complete the sentences with these words.**

about   apart   back   off   out   up

1 The bad weather set the trip _____ a week.
2 Joe's courage sets him _____ from others.
3 The explorers set _____ at dawn.
4 We didn't set _____ to break a record.
5 Let's set _____ camp for the night.
6 Once they reached the refuge, they set _____ preparing a meal.

## Lesson 3

## Vocabulary

Complete the table.

camper van    catamaran    dinghy    double-decker bus
glider    helicopter    jet ski    moped    rocket

| Water | Land | Air |
|-------|------|-----|
| _____ | _____ | _____ |
| _____ | _____ | _____ |
| _____ | _____ | _____ |

## Listening skills

**A  Look at the sentences in B and decide which speaker (1-4) will probably say sentences a-d below.**

a  We're going to have to speak to him about it. I don't think he understands just how dangerous it can be.  ☐

b  Can you believe it? She's only just turned sixteen.  ☐

c  I hadn't realised it would take over three hours to get back.  ☐

d  It really is the best way to travel.  ☐

**B  🎧 You will hear four people talking about travelling. Circle the correct answers.**

1  Speaker 1 didn't know the ferry / catamaran trip would take so long.

2  Speaker 2's favourite way of travelling is by camper van / plane.

3  Speaker 3 doesn't approve of helicopters / gliders.

4  Speaker 4 thinks Chantal is too young for a moped / bike.

## Listening task

🎧 You will hear two people talking about school presentations on means of transport. Which means of transport did each person talk about? For questions 1-5, write a letter (A-H) next to each person. There are three letters which you do not need to use.

1  Emily   ☐

2  Peter   ☐

3  Trevor  ☐

4  Lee     ☐

5  Dolores ☐

A  rockets

B  mopeds

C  catamarans

D  dinghies

E  gliders

F  double-decker buses

G  camper vans

H  helicopters

**Balancing arguments**

On the one hand, people choose/go on this kind of travel/holiday because …

In addition, this kind of holiday/journey/trip is popular with people who …

Another benefit/advantage of this kind of holiday journey/trip is …

Commuters/Holidaymakers/Tourists/Backpackers are also able to/can also …

On the other hand,/However, going on this kind of holiday/journey/trip means …

Another disadvantage/drawback is …

## Listen Up!

🎧 **Listen to a boy talking about a journey he went on and answer the questions.**

1  What kind of holiday is he talking about?

2  What positive points does he mention?

3  What negative points does he mention?

## Speaking skills

**A  Write A (advantages) or D (disadvantages).**

1  … allows you to … ☐
2  … keeps you fit … ☐
3  convenient ☐
4  dangerous ☐
5  environmentally friendly ☐
6  time consuming ☐
7  exhausting ☐
8  handy ☐
9  impractical ☐
10  inexpensive ☐
11  thrilling ☐
12  You don't get to … ☐
13  … exposed to bad weather … ☐
14  … breathe in polluted air … ☐

**B  Now work with a partner and use some of these words to discuss the advantages and disadvantages of:**

a  cycling as a hobby.

b  cycling to work.

## Speaking tasks

**A  Look at the pictures in B and make lists of as many advantages and disadvantages as you can think of that relate to them.**

**B  Work with a partner and take it in turns to describe what's happening in these pictures and talk about the reasons why people chose these kind of journeys. Student A should talk about picture 1 and Student B should talk about picture 2.**

**C  Now talk to your partner about which means of transport you prefer for both commuting and holidays. Explain your choices.**

## Adjectives

 One way of making informal writing more appealing is to use strong adjectives. You should try to use strong adjectives in all of your writing tasks, but it's important that you don't use them too much as this will make your writing seem overly exaggerated.

**Circle the strong adjectives.**

1 The airline's service was bad / terrible.
2 The scenery is nice / stunning in this part of the country.
3 The trip was very pleasant / good.
4 Our hotel was big / massive.
5 I was surprised / astounded by the travel guide's knowledge.

## Writing task

**A Read the writing task below and answer the questions.**

*Write an email inviting an English-speaking friend of yours to go on holiday with you and your family.*

1 Should the email be formal or informal?
2 How will the email begin?
3 What sort of information does your friend need to know?
4 How should you sign off?

**B Read the model email of invitation and replace the adjectives in bold with these strong adjectives.**

| delighted | exhausted | fascinating | hideous | luxury |

*model composition*

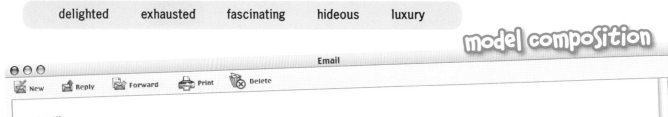

Hi Mike,

How are you? I'm getting ready for the summer holidays which begin soon. Mum and Dad have decided to go to Alaska this year and I was wondering if you could come with us. Are you doing anything at the beginning of July?

We're going for two weeks and we'll be staying at a **nice** hotel in the mountains. The flight takes about 15 hours so we'll be **tired** when we arrive. Mum says we'll take it easy the first few days and spend all our time using the hotel's facilities. I can't wait!

We're planning to go whale watching while we're there. I read an article on it and it sounds **interesting**. Humpback whales migrate 3,500 miles every year from Alaska to Hawaii and back again. By the time we get to Alaska they'll already have arrived so we can go on excursions in special boats to try to spot them.

I'll be **pleased** if you can come with us. Speak to your mum and dad about it and let me know soon if you'll be coming so we can book tickets. The cost of the trip including spending money should be around £1,000. Tell your parents the hotel is the complete opposite of the **ugly** one we stayed in last year.

Speak soon,

Bob

# Analyse it!

**Answer the questions.**

Which sentence

1 expresses an indirect invitation?
2 checks directly if the reader is available?
3 introduces an activity which they plan to do?
4 expresses the writer's wishes?
5 talks about how much they will have to pay?

# Writing plan

**Put the correct paragraph number from the model in each box.**

Paragraph ☐ Restate the invitation and tell your friend how you can make arrangements.

Paragraph ☐ Talk about one particular activity you can do there.

Paragraph ☐ Tell your friend your plans and invite him/her to join you.

Paragraph ☐ Give details about the journey and what you intend to do when you arrive.

# Grammar

## Future Tenses: review

**A Match.**

1 I'll be back before sunset.                a Future Simple
2 The plane's going to land in that field.   b Future Continuous
3 She'll be riding a white horse tomorrow.   c Future Perfect Simple
4 Will we have arrived by 9 o'clock?         d Future Perfect Continuous
5 I'll have been touring for months soon.    e Present Continuous for future
6 The train arrives at 6.30.                 f Present Simple for future
7 They're sailing to France on Friday.       g *be going to*

**B Which future tense(s) (a-g) from task A do we use to talk about:**

1 plans, and to predict something when we have proof or information?
2 things that will be in progress at a specific time?
3 an action that will have been completed before a specific time?
4 how long an action will have been in progress by a specific time?
5 programmed or timetabled events?
6 arrangements we've made for the near future?
7 offers, promises and warnings, and to make predictions?

**C Complete the sentences with the correct form of the verbs in brackets.**

1 I promise I _____ (come) on holiday with you.
2 I'm going to meet up with Jim while I _____ (be) in France.
3 By 10 pm, we _____ (travel) for 24 hours.
4 _____ (you/come) on the trip next week?
5 They _____ (fly) over Turkey at this time tomorrow.

# Writing task

*Write an email inviting an English-speaking friend of yours to go on an activity weekend with you and your family.*

## Write right!

**Use these steps to help you write your email.**

**Step 1** Underline the reason for writing the email in the Writing task.

**Step 2** Decide on details of the place/event you want to invite your friend to. Make notes about what you can do and see there.

**Step 3** Make a plan for your email and decide how you will organise your ideas. Use the plan opposite to help you.

**Step 4** Use your notes, your plan and the useful language above to write your email.

**Step 5** Read your email carefully when you have finished. Check that you have used strong adjectives, that your ideas are presented in a logical order and that you have written in the correct register.

**Discussion**

Discuss the reasons why people:

a go on expeditions to the poles.
b migrate to a different country.

# 6 Health and Fitness

Rock climbing is a difficult and dangerous sport that requires a high level of physical strength and fitness, plus mental calm and control.

The sport started about 200 years ago in Colorado, USA. Climbing has played an important part in exploration in the last two centuries, with many historical 'firsts' and world records. These include the first successful climb of the world's highest mountain, Mount Everest, by Sherpa Tensing Norgay and Edmund Hillary. In 1980, Reinhold Messner became the first man to climb Mount Everest alone.

## Quiz

**When was the first successful climb of Mount Everest?**

a  1953
b  1876
c  1925

**Discussion**

'Keeping fit and healthy is expensive and takes up too much time.' Discuss.

## Reading

**Read the fact sheet about the activity pyramid. How often must you do an aerobic activity?**

# The Activity Pyramid

Improve and maintain your fitness through physical activity. Use the activity pyramid to get the balance right.

Sedentary activities: as few as possible

Strength-building activities: 2-3 times a week

Aerobic and recreational activities: 3-5 times a week

Everyday activities: as often as possible

### Everyday activities

These are the kind of activities that you have to do most to keep fit, so they appear at the bottom of the pyramid. In fact, you must try to do them as often as possible because everyday activities can make a big difference to your general fitness. They include doing light housework like sweeping the floor or tidying your room, walking up the stairs instead of taking the lift or escalator and playing outdoors. (1) _____ You needn't buy special equipment or sign up for classes to do them.

### Aerobic & recreational activities

Young people tend to enjoy this kind of activity more than any other. Playing basketball, football and games in the playground as well as swimming, riding a bike and skipping all fall into this category. These aerobic activities help to pump oxygen round the body and exercise the heart as well as other muscles. (2) _____ To stay in shape, you must aim to do an aerobic activity 3-5 times per week as shown on the pyramid.

### Strength-building activities

These activities help you strengthen your muscles and become more flexible. (3) _____ Alternatively, you could try out the more strenuous things in an adventure playground like rope climbing and the monkey bars. These activities come further up in the pyramid and they're recommended 2-3 times per week in order to stay on form.

### Sedentary activities

Playing computer games and watching your favourite TV show can be easy and entertaining ways to pass your time. (4) _____ This is why they appear right at the top of the pyramid. Unless you watch your favourite reality show while cleaning the windows, or dance and do stretching exercises while listening to music, then this is the kind of thing you must try to cut down on. (5) _____ Then you could suggest that you decide on one day a week when you will all make an effort to keep the TV and the computer off all day.

## Comprehension

**Complete the fact sheet with these sentences.**

a  Do you and your family spend most of your free time being inactive?

b  They include martial arts of all kinds, stretching and yoga.

c  They also burn up energy quickly and help you to control your weight.

d  In other words, they're simple actions that we're all able to do every day.

e  However, they don't do much for your physical fitness.

## Vocabulary

**Circle the correct words.**

1  Going jogging can help you burn / sign up calories.

2  I must cut down on / fall into the number of hours I watch TV.

3  How can I strengthen / recommend my arms?

4  What skips / pumps oxygen around the body?

5  Karen is a gymnast so she's very inactive / flexible.

6  Which category / escalator does cycling come in?

# Grammar

## Modals 1: Can, could, be able to, would, have to, must, needn't

| Use | Example |
|---|---|
| Ability/Possibility | We can go to the pool after school.<br>Tim could swim when he was a toddler.<br>Were you able to fix his broken tooth? |
| Requests/Suggestions | Can I read your book on nutrition?<br>Would you ask the coach to call me?<br>We could eat salad instead.<br>Could you leave me to sleep in? |
| Asking for permission | Can we go to the leisure centre?<br>Could you show me how to dive? |
| Giving/Refusing permission | Yes, you can./No, you can't. |
| Deduction | This can't be mine. It's too small.<br>This must be Mum's equipment. |
| Necessity/Obligation | Carla must see the doctor.<br>We have to look after ourselves. |
| Prohibition | She mustn't stop eating fruit. |
| Lack of necessity/obligation | You don't have to pay for the gym.<br>We needn't take these pills. |

**Note:** We can't use could to talk about specific situations in the past which happened only once; we must use was/were able to instead. However, we can use couldn't to talk about specific situations in the past.
*I was able to run across the street to catch the bus.*
*I couldn't eat the food she served.*

---

**A** The words in bold are wrong. Write the correct words. Sometimes more than one answer is possible.

1 Do we **must** take part in the aerobics class? _____

2 You **can't** go to hospital; it isn't necessary. _____

3 **Can** he able to do the marathon? _____

4 Jack **could** give me some advice yesterday. _____

5 'Can I borrow your ball, please?' 'No, you **don't have to**.' _____

6 I hate aerobics because it **could** be very tiring. _____

7 That **needn't** be Sally running on the track. She's broken her leg. _____

8 **Need** you help me do this exercise, please? _____

**B** Look at the pictures and complete the sentences with a suitable modal verb. Sometimes more than one answer is possible.

1 You _____ dive into the swimming pool.

2 We _____ take the lift because there are stairs.

3 _____ you hold this for a minute?

4 They _____ change their eating habits.

## Collocations

Choose the correct answers.

1 Going to the gym helps me stay on _____ .
  a fit    b shape    c form

2 How can I control my _____ ?
  a weight    b kilos    c figure

3 What can I do to maintain physical _____?
  a health    b fitness    c effort

4 Sam's having a _____ at the doctor's today.
  a push-up    b warm-up    c check-up

5 He can't get to the _____ of the problem.
  a basis    b foundation    c root

6 Training regularly keeps athletes at their _____ .
  a top    b peak    c height

## Speaking

Work with a partner and suggest ways young people can make their lifestyles healthier. One of you can talk about keeping fit and the other about having a healthy diet. Use can, could, be able to, must, have to and needn't.

## Writing

Write two short paragraphs using your ideas from the Speaking task.

**Discussion**

'You are what you eat.' Discuss.

## Reading

**Read the article about food labelling. What does an amber 'traffic light' on a package refer to?**

# What's that you're eating?

Nutrition is extremely important for our well-being. Without a proper diet our bodies can't function properly and we are more prone to sickness and poor general health. While many people are aware of this, what is not so clear is exactly what people ought to eat – and to avoid – to ensure that they are eating healthily.

This issue is particularly important in modern times as eating convenience foods has been popular for decades now. Our busy lifestyles have meant that we have less time to spend in the kitchen and so we frequently buy ready meals. However, more and more people are having health problems as a result of consuming these products as they are often high in sugar, salt, fat and calories. For this reason, food manufacturers have been told they must print nutritional information about the content of a product on packaging so that people can compare similar products and make healthier choices. Moreover, manufacturers' obligation to provide this information gives them a reason to produce healthier products that people will prefer. Information like whether a product contains gluten, nuts and dairy products is also detailed because large numbers of people are allergic to or intolerant of these substances.

But might this labelling be creating greater insecurity concerning food? Some people think advertising what is in a product may create more confusion about what the best thing to eat is, especially if different businesses use a variety of ways to display the information.

So how should manufacturers label food so that people can make the best choices and avoid confusion? Research has shown that a 'traffic light' system on the front of packs is a simple and effective method. Ingredients which are unhealthy if too much is consumed – specifically fat, sugar and salt – are colour coded, with green indicating none or very little of the substance, amber for a medium amount and red for a large amount per serving. The number of calories in a serving is usually on the back of the pack. This system is easy for consumers to understand and enables them to get an idea of the overall 'healthiness' of a product at a glance.

**Guess what!**

Polythene, the most common type of plastic used for packaging, was discovered by accident in England in 1932.

## Comprehension

**Write A if the sentence is correct and B if it is not correct.**

1 People with poor nutrition are more likely to suffer from poor health. ☐

2 The people who eat convenience foods don't have time to cook. ☐

3 Many people can't eat foods that contain cheese and milk. ☐

4 Not everybody thinks food labelling is a good idea. ☐

5 The 'traffic light' system calls for information about calories on the front of packs. ☐

6 'Traffic light' labelling is confusing for most consumers. ☐

## Vocabulary

**Find the words in the text and circle the correct meaning, a or b.**

1 diet
  a eating habits
  b way to lose weight

2 issue
  a copy of a publication
  b important topic

3 consuming
  a eating
  b using

4 intolerant
  a prejudiced
  b sensitive

5 glance
  a a hit
  b a quick look

# Grammar

## Modals 2: May, might, should, ought to

| Use | Example |
| --- | --- |
| Possibility | Carol may become a fitness instructor. The dietician might suggest some changes. |
| Asking for permission | May I take a look at your throat? |
| Giving permission | You may not have another biscuit. |
| Giving advice | You should have a check-up. They ought not to eat so much fried food. |
| Prediction | He should win the race. |

**Note:** We don't use the question forms of ought to or might.

**A** Underline the examples of **may, might, should and ought to** in the article. What does each example express?

**B** Rewrite the sentences using the words given.

1 It's possible that Jim will take up yoga.
   **might**
   Jim _____ yoga.

2 You don't eat enough vegetables.
   **should**
   You _____ vegetables.

3 It's possible that garlic is good for you.
   **may**
   Garlic _____ good for you.

4 Why don't they go on a first-aid course?
   **to**
   They _____ on a first-aid course.

5 Is it a good idea for me to eat fish?
   **I**
   _____ fish?

6 You worry too much about your weight.
   **ought**
   You _____ so much about your weight.

# Vocabulary

**Write the correct words.**

> dairy products    nutritional information    nuts
> packets of food    ready meal    supplements

_____  _____  _____

  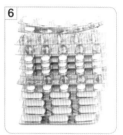

_____  _____  _____

# Listening

🎧 **Listen and number the issues in the order they will be presented.**

a first aid ☐
b physical fitness ☐
c personal hygiene ☐
d nutrition ☐
e question time ☐
f aches and pains ☐

## Prepositions

**Match.**

| | |
| --- | --- |
| 1 Some people are allergic | a from drowning. |
| 2 This advice doesn't apply | b from getting ill. |
| 3 Vaccination can prevent people | c to gluten. |
| 4 Some people are prone | d from poor health. |
| 5 I saved her | e to heart patients. |
| 6 My sister suffers | f to getting colds. |

65

## Vocabulary

**Complete the sentences with these words.**

| burn | consume | digest |
|------|---------|--------|
| nibble | nourish | supplement |

1 Do you think I should take vitamin pills to _____ my diet?

2 Leave time to _____ your food before doing strenuous activities.

3 Vitamins and minerals are necessary to _____ your body.

4 We ought not to _____ on unhealthy snacks between meals.

5 We shouldn't _____ more food than we need.

6 Is jogging a good way to _____ calories?

## Listening skills

**A** 🎧 **Listen to the dialogue and draw items that are mentioned in the boxes.**

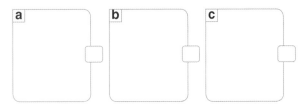

**B** **Which of the drawings is the *least* likely to be the correct answer to the question below?**

What does the woman recommend that the man should eat?

**C** 🎧 **Now listen again and tick (✓) the picture which *best* answers the question in B.**

## Listening task

🎧 **Listen and tick (✓) the correct pictures.**

1 What does the boy want to eat?

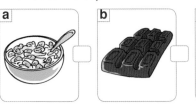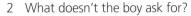

a    b    c

2 What doesn't the boy ask for?

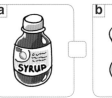  

3 Which ingredients does the recipe say ought not to be used?

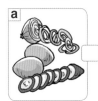  

4 What time must the girl be at the sports centre?

5 Which talk might the man attend?

6 What does the man suggest the woman should do?

  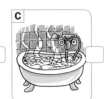

### Agreeing

Yes, I totally/completely/entirely agree with you.
I think you're right./You're absolutely right about …
That's exactly what I think.
I see what you mean.
I couldn't agree more.

### Disagreeing

I'm not sure that's a good idea.
I don't think that's the best option.
I'm afraid I don't agree.
I think it'd be better if/to …

### Conceding a point

You've got a point, but …
I see what you're saying, but …
I agree to a certain extent, but …

## Listen Up!

🎧 **Listen to Simon and Ella doing the following speaking task and answer the questions.**

*Your friend's eleven-year-old son would like to lose some weight and your friend has asked you and your partner for advice on how he can do this. Discuss various options and recommend one activity that you think he should do.*

1  Which expressions from *Express Yourself!* does each student use?

2  What arguments and counterarguments do they present for each choice?

3  What do they finally agree on?

## Speaking skills

A  **Look at the task in C. Which student will give advice to the other one? How can you start the dialogue?**

B  **Look at the photo below. Who do you think is Student A and who is Student B from task C?**

C  **Work with a partner and role play a dialogue between two friends. One of you should be Student A and the other Student B. Use this information and the phrases from *Express Yourself!* to help you.**

| Student A | Student B |
|---|---|
| *You want to lose weight and have decided to eat only fruit and not to exercise.* | *Your friend wants to lose weight and has decided to eat only fruit and not to exercise.* |
| • low calories | • not balanced diet |
| • no fat | • need for proteins and some fat |
| • high in vitamins | • physical exercise important |

## Speaking tasks

A  **Read the Speaking task in B and look at the pictures. Talk to your partner about what suggestion each picture shows and then rank them from 1-5, with 1 being the most helpful and 5 being the least helpful.**

1  _____
2  _____
3  _____
4  _____
5  _____

B  **Your friend has been feeling very tired lately and doesn't have much energy. Look at the pictures below and work with your partner to talk about the kind of changes she could make to her lifestyle in order to feel better. Decide which two things are the most helpful.**

## Capturing and keeping readers' interest

> Writers of features for magazines try to ensure that their articles are read from the beginning to the end. In order to do this, they include special language features which are designed to make the writing more interesting. These include directly addressing the reader, asking rhetorical questions for effect and using imperatives.

**Write DA (direct address), RQ (rhetorical question) or I (imperative) next to these sentences. There may be more than one answer in each case.**

1 Do you ever feel guilty about the foods you eat? _____

2 Before you rush out to buy a miracle cure, see your doctor. _____

3 If you're one of those people who hates physical exercise, then read on. _____

4 What's the point in having the perfect figure if it doesn't bring happiness? _____

5 Is nibbling on a chocolate bar more appealing to you than eating fruit? _____

6 You should take time to prepare nutritious meals with fresh ingredients. _____

## Writing task

**A Read this writing task and answer the questions.**

*Write an article for your school magazine about a health issue concerning young people.*

1 Who will read the article?

2 Are you given a specific issue to write about or will you decide what to focus on?

**B Read the model article and underline examples of direct address, rhetorical questions and imperatives.**

model composition

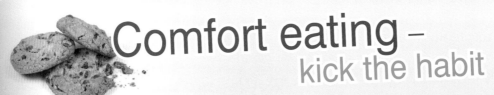
Comfort eating – kick the habit

Have you ever felt anxious about something and tried to make yourself feel better by consuming a snack which is high in calories and fat? We all know that we need to eat properly and to cut out unhealthy foods. How easy is it, though, to maintain a balanced diet when we have lots of demands on us?

The benefits of a healthy diet which is rich in vitamins and minerals and low in fat are widely known. However, pressures like exams and arguments with friends or family can lead young people to have problems with their diet. The odd chocolate bar doesn't do any harm, but people who regularly use food as a reward or punishment may have developed a bad habit.

Comfort eating may make people feel better in the short term, but it doesn't provide a solution to the problem. When you find yourself saying 'I shouldn't have eaten that.' think about how you could have dealt with the real problem and ask for help if necessary.

Eating is a very important part of our lives. However, we all need to develop a healthy relationship with food and resist the temptation to eat for comfort.

# Analyse it!

**Tick (✓) the things the writer has done in the article.**

1 provided a headline ☐
2 used very informal language ☐
3 written about one main health issue ☐
4 chosen a health issue relevant to young people ☐
5 given advice ☐

# Writing plan

**Complete the plan for the model article with these sentences.**

> a Analyse the nature of the problem.
> b Comfort eating – kick the habit
> c Introduce issue to be discussed and make some general comments about it.
> d Provide specific advice on how to deal with the problem.
> e Sum up and give general advice about the issue.

Headline _____
Paragraph 1 _____
Paragraph 2 _____
Paragraph 3 _____
Paragraph 4 _____

# Grammar

### Modals 3: perfect forms

We can use modal verbs with have and the past participle to talk about past actions and states.

| | |
|---|---|
| Possibility | She may/might have gone to see the doctor. He could have broken the record. |
| Deduction | You can't have done aerobics in the 1950s. It must have been a steps class you did. |
| Criticism | They shouldn't have eaten all the cake. He was sleeping when he ought to have been exercising. |

**Note:** *We could have injured ourselves badly.* talks about something that was possible in the past, but didn't happen. *The medicine may/might have helped him.* talks about something that was possible in the past but we don't know whether it happened or not.

**Circle the correct words.**

1 They could have **told / tell** us the cake contained nuts.
2 He ought not to **have / have been** drunk the dirty water.
3 It can't **be / have been** Jane at the pool yesterday. She's in France.
4 Rob **could / might** have scored a goal, but he fell.
5 Should we have **watched / watch** the first-aid video?
6 Jane **can't / must** have been on a diet because she's lost weight.

# Writing task

*Write an article for a school magazine advising students on how to keep fit.*

## Write right!

**Use these steps to help you write your article.**

**Step 1** Underline the key words in the Writing task.

**Step 2** Make a list of possible ways students could keep fit and then chose two or three that you will focus on.

**Step 3** Make notes about the advantages of the activities you have chosen. Think about matters such as the benefits they bring, who they appeal to and how much they cost.

**Step 4** Make a plan for your article and decide on an appropriate headline. Use the plan opposite to help you.

**Step 5** Use your notes, your plan and the useful language above to write your article.

**Step 6** Edit your article when you have finished to check you have used direct address, rhetorical questions and imperatives.

## Discussion

'We face many health threats every day.' How far is this true regarding:

a the food we eat?

b illnesses?

**69**

# Review 3

## Vocabulary

### A Circle the correct words.

1 Do you suffer / prevent from any allergies?

2 I believe that travel tolerates / broadens your mind.

3 That huge ice floe is drifting / ingenious.

4 You need a lot of determination / effort to break a record.

5 You must ensure / enable that you have your passport.

6 Her skills set her apart / back from the other team members.

### B Write the correct words.

| dinghy | double-decker bus | globe |
| ingredients | monkey bars | packet |

1

2

_____  _____

3

4

_____  _____

5

6

_____  _____

### C Choose the correct answers.

1 I'm trying to _____ on the amount of chocolate I eat.
   a cut down
   b set off
   c set back

2 Are you _____ to illness?
   a intolerant
   b prone
   c flexible

3 We completed the marathon against all _____ .
   a limitations
   b odds
   c accomplishments

4 _____ like milk and cheese don't stay fresh for long.
   a Ready meals
   b Convenience foods
   c Dairy products

5 Janine is always _____ herself to the limits.
   a battling
   b pumping
   c testing

### D Match.

1 You must work out to stay    a her weight.

2 My parents lead    b sedentary lives.

3 Try to kick    c the balance right.

4 Anne's trying to control    d in shape.

5 With diet it's hard to get    e calories.

6 Walking is a good way to burn    f your bad habits.

## Grammar

**A The words in bold are wrong. Write the correct words.**

1  Stop! You **don't must** eat that! _____

2  Will you **can** come with me? _____

3  Oh no! That car **will** crash into us! _____

4  I'm not sure but I **should** go out. _____

5  She might **had** forgotten. _____

6  They'll have been **run** for hours soon. _____

**B Rearrange the words to make sentences.**

1  will / ship / from / be / here / sailing / this

2  have / you / yesterday / gone / jogging / could

3  ? / Fred / a / going / travel / on / plane / is / to

4  noon / left / we / have / gym / will / the / by

5  ? / fitter / by / summer / she / be / will

6  ? / borrow / on / book / may / your / expeditions / Clara

**C Match.**

a  He must avoid the other ship. ☐

b  He is going to dive into the water. ☐

c  He should have a drink of water. ☐

d  He ought to have put his hat on. ☐

e  He may fall down the hatch. ☐

f  He will be eating fish for dinner. ☐

## Strange but true!

**Match these strange but true stories with their pictures.**

**1** ☐ A famous celebrity drinks two tablespoons of apple vinegar every day. She says it helps to remove fat from the body and stops her eating junk food.

**2** ☐ A 90 year-old woman from Okinawa says eating seaweed has allowed her to live a long life. Every day she collects her own fresh seaweed from the beach near her house.

**3** ☐ In Kentucky, USA, everybody must take a bath once a year by law.

| a | b | c |
|---|---|---|
|  | 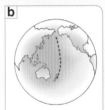 |  |

| d | e | f |
|---|---|---|
|  |  |  |

**4** ☐ A seabird called the Sooty Shearwater migrates nearly 64,000 kilometres every summer from New Zealand to the North Pacific Ocean to look for food.

**5** ☐ Fumiyasu Yamakawa does yoga every day because he wants to stay in shape for the yearly decathlon which he takes part in. His favourite events are the pole vault and the long jump. Fumiyasu is a very young 85 year-old.

**6** ☐ Some schools organise Walk to School Weeks for their students. They encourage students to give up the school bus or their parents' cars for one week in the year and walk all the way to school. Some schools even offer them a healthy breakfast when they arrive.

# 7 Planet Earth

## Quiz

**What percentage of the Earth's surface is covered by water?**

a   about 27 %

b   about 54 %

c   about 71 %

This picture shows NASA astronaut Bruce McCandless. McCandless was the first person to go on an untethered spacewalk when he 'flew' about 100 metres away from the spaceship Challenger in February 1984. He was able to do this because of a special jet backpack called the MMU which was used on only three missions and then taken out of service due to safety concerns. From this point above the surface of the Earth, the blue oceans and the clouds in the atmosphere are clearly visible and contrast with the blackness of space. McCandless is one of a very small group of people who have seen our planet from this point of view.

## Reading

Do the quiz to find out if you're a beginner, a mover or a high flyer when it comes to geography. What is the maximum number of points you can get?

# Planet Earth Quiz

**Are you a high flyer when it comes to geography or is knowledge of our planet not one of your strong points? Do the quiz to find out.**

1 How many countries are there in the world?
   a  more than 250
   b  around 190
   c  less than 100

2 How many islands does the UK (England, Scotland, Northern Ireland and Wales) have?
   a  less than 100
   b  around 2,000
   c  more than 6,000

3 Which of the following languages has the most native speakers in the world?
   a  Mandarin Chinese
   b  English
   c  Spanish

4 What is the capital of Canada?
   a  Ottowa
   b  Toronto
   c  Canberra

5 What is Europe's largest city?
   a  Moscow
   b  London
   c  Berlin

6 What is the population of the Earth?
   a  less than 4 billion
   b  over 6.5 billion
   c  about 9 billion

**Now look at the answers below and score two points for every correct answer. Then read on to see what your score means.**

**Beginners (2-4 points)**
If you score 2-4, geography isn't your strong point. Unless you enjoy knowing nothing about the planet, you'll have to do a bit more reading on the subject to improve your knowledge. Check out the National Geographic Kids' site. It's full of interesting articles as well as facts and figures about our world that will help you brush up your knowledge.

**Movers (6-8 points)**
If you score 6-8, you know your way around the globe, but there are still some points that you need to work on. You might want to refresh your memory on geographical knowledge. If you do a little more research, you'll soon be up to scratch.

**High Flyers (10-12 points)**
If you score 10-12, congratulations! If there was a prize for geographical knowledge, you would win it! You excel at the subject and are very interested in all matters to do with planet Earth. You're a high flyer and if you don't know something, you'll stop at nothing until you find out the answer.

1b 2c 3a 4a 5a 6b

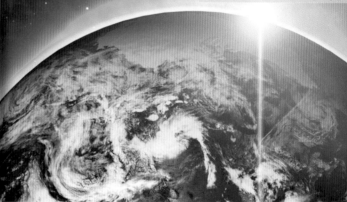

## Comprehension

Write B (beginner), M (mover) or F (flyer). Who

1  is thirsty for knowledge? ☐

2  could benefit most from extra reading? ☐

3  is fascinated by planet Earth? ☐

4  has a good grasp of geography with a few weak points? ☐

5  is probably not interested in geography? ☐

6  is advised to use the Internet? ☐

## Vocabulary

Find words or phrases in the quiz which mean the same as the words in bold. The words and phrases are in the same order as they are in the text.

1  Geography is **the thing you're good at.** _____

2  Do you want to **know more**? _____

3  I use text books **in addition to** the Internet. _____

4  I think you should **revise** capital cities. _____

5  You'll be **good enough** if you study. _____

6  I'll **do everything I can** to find out. _____

# Grammar

We use the zero conditional to talk about things that always happen.
*If you leave lights on, you waste energy.*

> **Note:** We can use when instead of if with the zero conditional.
> *When the sun goes down, it gets dark.*

We use the first conditional to talk about things that are likely to happen in the present or in the future.
*What will happen if birth rates continue to rise?*

> **Note:** We can use unless with the first conditional to mean if not.
> *Unless we act now, the planet will be destroyed.*

We use the second conditional to talk about something that is impossible in the present or the future; to talk about something that is possible, but is unlikely to happen in the present or the future; and to give advice.
*If the Earth was flat, we would fall off the edge.*
*I'd be surprised if Sydney was made the capital of Australia.*
*If I were you, I would buy a more up-to-date atlas.*

**A Complete the sentences with the correct form of the verbs in brackets.**

1 I _____ (visit) Brighton if I lived in the UK.

2 When there's a full moon, the stars _____ (not be) clear.

3 If you were rich, _____ (you/donate) money for environmental research?

4 Unless we _____ (act) now, more damage will be done.

5 There _____ (be) less pollution if we use our cars less.

**B Rewrite the sentences using the words given.**

1 If we don't help them, many species will disappear.
   **unless**
   Many species will disappear _____ them.

2 You should brush up your knowledge.
   **were**
   If _____, I would brush up my knowledge.

3 If you have a bath, recycle the water.
   **when**
   Recycle the water _____ .

4 Don't cut down those trees because it's against the law.
   **if**
   You'll break the law _____ those trees.

5 We won't go swimming unless the weather improves.
   **improve**
   If _____, we won't go swimming.

# Word formation

**A Complete the table.**

| Verb | Noun | Adjective |
|---|---|---|
| (1) _____ | excellence | excellent |
| populate | (2) _____ | populated |
| research | (3) _____ | researched |
| (4) _____ | prediction | predictable |
| – | extinction | (5) _____ |
| emit | (6) _____ | emitted |

**B Complete the sentences with some of the words from A.**

1 Scientists still can't _____ earthquakes accurately.

2 Power stations _____ a lot of pollution.

3 Fourteen million people live in Mumbai, making it the world's most _____ city.

4 This report on the Nile is very well _____ .

5 What can we do to prevent the _____ of endangered species?

6 The documentary on conservation won an award for _____ .

# Speaking

**Choose a country with your partner and talk about the following things.**

1 What is the population?

2 What is the capital?

3 Which are the two biggest cities?

4 What is the climate like?

5 What is beautiful about the country?

6 What environmental problems does the country suffer from? How can these be solved?

# Writing

**Write a short fact sheet about the country you spoke about in the Speaking task. Use subheadings to help you organise your information.**

## Reading

**Read the article about photovoltaic energy. How does this system create energy?**

# Photovoltaic energy –
### just a bright idea or a practical solution?

Global warming is a sad fact that we have to face up to. Decades of burning fossil fuels and using nuclear power has been catastrophic for our environment. Much of the destruction of nature that we have seen in the last century would not have taken place if these methods had not been used. Apart from this, the fact that the Earth is running out of fossil fuels means that we have no choice but to look for alternative energy sources.

The burning question is, what kind of alternative energy should we use? There are several, but photovoltaic energy, which involves the conversion of light from the sun into electricity, is one of the most promising. Electricity is generated when sunlight hits the photovoltaic cells on specially designed panels. This process of converting sunlight into electricity has massive benefits for our planet. The environment is not polluted in order to produce it, it causes no noise, and it uses a renewable source as sunlight will never run out.

At the moment, photovoltaic energy is popular in remote areas where there is no access to an electricity grid, but it is also used as a green alternative by some homes and businesses that are connected to the grid. Unfortunately, the small number of people who use this form of energy means photovoltaic equipment is expensive. But if demand increases, then prices will drop. In some countries, rather than wish citizens would turn to photovoltaic energy on their own, governments have established photovoltaic programmes to give people an incentive to adopt it.

Apart from the cost, another drawback of photovoltaic energy is that the efficiency of the panels depends on their location – the sunnier the place, the more efficient they are. Don't despair, though, and think 'If only I lived on the equator!' if you live in Norway. Even in countries which see little sunlight, sufficient energy can be generated if the panels are placed in the correct position and tilted towards the sun.

So is the future photovoltaic? Scientists predict that by 2030 these systems will supply 14% of our energy needs. If this came true, it would be good news for our planet and good news for future generations too.

**Guess what!**
*Light from the sun takes about eight minutes to reach Earth.*

## Comprehension

**Write A if the sentence is correct and B if it is incorrect.**

1 We started using nuclear power during the last decade. ☐
2 We can't keep on using fossil fuels forever. ☐
3 Photovoltaic energy doesn't cause pollution. ☐
4 Only people not connected to the electricity grid can use photovoltaic energy. ☐
5 Photovoltaic equipment will get cheaper if more people buy it. ☐
6 Photovoltaic panels cannot be used in Norway. ☐

## Vocabulary

**Find words or phrases in the article that have these meanings. The words and phrases are in the same order as they appear in the text.**

1 disastrous _____
2 occurred _____
3 changing something into another form _____
4 network _____
5 lose hope _____
6 placed with one side higher than the other _____

# Grammar

## Third conditional

We use the third conditional to talk about things that were possible in the past, but didn't happen. It is used to talk about hypothetical situations or actions.
*If we had predicted the hurricane, lives would have been saved.*

## Wish and if only

We use wish and if only to talk about a situation or action that we regret or want to change.

We use wish/if only + Past Simple to talk about the present or the future.
*I wish my house had photovoltaic energy.*
*If only more people cared about the environment.*

We use wish/if only + Past Perfect Simple or Past Perfect Continuous to talk about the past.
*Shelley wishes she hadn't wasted so much electricity.*
*If only he hadn't been chasing the tornado.*

We use wish/if only + would to talk about an annoying action someone else has done or to talk about an action we want to change in the future.
*I wish companies would reduce the price of these panels.*
*If only they would ban factories from polluting the environment.*

Note: We never use wish/if only + would to talk about our own behaviour.

**A  Look at the sentence highlighted in the article and answer the questions.**

1  Which conditional is used?

2  What has happened in the last century?

3  What could we have done to prevent the destruction of nature?

**B  Circle the correct words.**

1  If she'd known / knew about the fire, she wouldn't have gone to the forest.

2  If only we had cleaned / would clean the beach!

3  I wish we lived / had lived in the country. Can't we move?

4  I would have helped / helped Dad fix the panels if he had asked me.

5  Jane wishes she hasn't been / hadn't been looking at the sun.

**C  Complete the sentences with your own words.**

1  If only the environment ... .

2  If we had prevented the damage earlier, ... .

3  I wish our government ... .

4  If they hadn't put out the fire, ... .

5  If only all citizens ... .

# Vocabulary

**Match.**

| | | | |
|---|---|---|---|
| 1 | Is nuclear | a | organic farm? |
| 2 | Coal is a | b | power a bad idea? |
| 3 | Wind power is a | c | green alternative. |
| 4 | Is sunlight a | d | fossil fuel. |
| 5 | I'm a member of a | e | buyers' cooperative. |
| 6 | Is this an | f | renewable source of energy? |

# Listening

🎧 **Listen to an environmental group's discussion about their plan of action. Tick (✓) the correct boxes.**

Plan of action:

|  | Green Team | Red Team |
|---|---|---|
| 1 city centre protest | ☐ | ☐ |
| 2 recycling | ☐ | ☐ |
| 3 farmers' market | ☐ | ☐ |
| 4 clean up the beach | ☐ | ☐ |
| 5 clean up office | ☐ | ☐ |

## Phrasal Verbs

**Complete the sentences with the correct form of these phrasal verbs.**

| bring about | carry out | catch on |
|---|---|---|
| face up to | run out | turn to |

1  We're _____ a survey on global warming this week.

2  When is oil predicted to _____?

3  They decided to _____ another form of energy.

4  What _____ yesterday's disaster?

5  The government has got to _____ its responsibilities.

6  Do you think that photovoltaic panels will _____?

## Vocabulary

Circle the correct answers.

| Problems | Causes | Solutions |
|---|---|---|
| **dam / environmental** pollution | **water / natural** disaster | **natural / green** alternative |
| **global / population** warming | **proper / high** consumption | **dam / population** construction |
| **water / green** shortage | **population / global** explosion | **high / proper** management |

## Listening skills

**A** Work with a partner and take it in turns to read the figures in B below out loud.

**B** 🎧 Listen and circle the numbers you hear.

| | | | | | | | | |
|---|---|---|---|---|---|---|---|---|
| 1 | a | 1,000 | b | 1,000,000 | c | 1,000,000,000 |
| 2 | a | ½ | b | ⅓ | c | ¼ |
| 3 | a | 13 | b | 30 | c | 33 |
| 4 | a | 2006 | b | 2060 | c | 2016 |
| 5 | a | 7.5 | b | 75 | c | 7½ |

## Listening task

Listen to the talk on a radio programme about water shortages and complete the notes.

**Causes of drought:**
increases in temperature and world's (1) _____

**By 2025:**
about (2) _____ of world's people will suffer drought

**Previous century:**
water consumption increased (3) _____

**Solutions:**
reduce consumption and have proper (4) _____ of water

**Number of dams:**
(5) _____ built in Indian villages

**Working for Water:**
water is (6) _____ for those who show that they're conserving it

## express yourself!

### Predicting

If people continue/carry on + -ing …, there'll …

Unless people stop + -ing, there'll …

If we don't take action, it'll …

Unless we take action, it'll …

… might/may/will result in + -ing/noun …

… might/may/will lead to + bare infinitive/noun …

## Listen Up!

🎧 **Listen to someone talking about water fountains and answer the questions.**

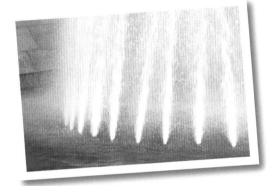

1  Which phrases from *Express Yourself!* does the speaker use?

2  Does the speaker present logical arguments?

3  Which word best describes the speaker's tone of voice?
   a  amused
   b  sarcastic
   c  furious

4  Does this make his arguments more or less convincing?

5  What could he do to be taken more seriously?

## Speaking skills

**A  Look at the pictures below and take it in turns to discuss with a partner how they make you feel and why.**

**B  Predict with your partner what might be the consequences of the situations in the pictures. Use the phrases from *Express Yourself!* and make sure you maintain a calm tone of voice.**

## Speaking tasks

**A  Read the words and phrases below with your partner. Write F for the ones that relate to floods, C for the ones that relate to chopping down trees, B for ones that relate to both and N for the ones that relate to neither.**

1  causing air pollution          _____

2  clearing forests               _____

3  damage to property             _____

4  destruction of natural environment  _____

5  destroying natural habitats    _____

6  increased rainfall             _____

7  making land available for cattle  _____

8  water level                    _____

**B  Work with a partner and take it in turns to describe these pictures and talk about how they might relate to environmental problems. Student A should talk about picture 1 and Student B should talk about picture 2.**

**C  Discuss what we can do in our everyday lives to reduce the negative effects we have on the environment.**

79

## Linking words and phrases 1

 We use linking words in our writing to make it flow better. As, since and because show the reason why something happens. Also, as well, and, too and as well as join different ideas that are related in some way. Like, such as, for example and for instance give examples, but only for example and for instance can be used at the start of a new sentence.

**Complete the sentences with one of the words or phrases from the box on the left. Sometimes more than one answer is possible.**

1 We have to consume less water _____ there'll be a shortage if we don't.

2 Students _____ parents can help with the project.

3 Many people now use green alternatives _____ they recognise their benefits.

4 We will be recycling and cleaning up the beach _____ .

5 There are lots of green things you can do. _____ , you can use less water.

# Writing task

**A  Read the writing task below and answer the questions.**

*Imagine you are a member of your school's environmental group,* Clean Up Nature, *and you have been asked to write a report on the group. Write a report informing teachers and students about what has been done so far and what could be done in the future.*

1  What have you been asked to write?

2  What register will you use?

3  How many things do you have to write about?

4  What are they?

**B  Read the model report and circle the correct words.**

*model composition*

# REPORT on the Clean Up Nature group

### Introduction

The aim of this report is to review the activities of Pinewood High's environmental group, *Clean Up Nature*. It will discuss what the group has already achieved (1) and / too make suggestions for future action.

### Achievements so far

The recycling scheme began three months ago and the group has already achieved a lot. (2) Such as / For example, recycling bins have been placed in the school playground. Students were informed at a meeting about which objects can be recycled (3) as well as / also which bin materials go in. This was very successful (4) as well as / since most students now use the bins properly.

### Future projects

• One project that the group could do is clean up the local forest. We must take action if we want to prevent future forest fires. Students would help pick up the rubbish and recycle or dispose of it (5) well / too.

• Another task we could take on is the creation of materials (6) such / like posters to increase students' awareness of environmental issues. We could also create a web page if we were given access to the school's computer room.

### Conclusion

In conclusion, we have already achieved a lot but there is still much more that we can do. If we continue to work together, we will be successful in making a difference to our environment.

# Analyse it!

**Answer the questions.**

1  Which project has the environmental group already started?
2  How do we know it has been worthwhile?
3  How has the writer presented the two possible future projects?
4  What will the group need to create the web page?
5  What does the writer say the key to success is?

# Writing plan

**The words in bold are wrong. Write the correct words to complete the paragraph plan.**

Title: Report on the *Clean Up Nature* group

Paragraph 1: Introduction: **Conclude** the topic and talk about the reason it has been written.

Paragraph 2: Achievements so far: Talk about a project already **finished**, say what has been done and how its **failure** has been measured.

Paragraph 3: Projects for the future: Suggest a future project and explain **when** it should be done.

Paragraph 4: Suggest another project and give a reason for your choice.

Paragraph 5: Conclusion: Make a **first** statement.

# Grammar

## Conditionals with modal verbs

We can use modal verbs in first, second and third conditional sentences.

In first conditional sentences we can use can, could, will, would, should, ought to, might, must and needn't + bare infinitive in the result clause.
*If you want to help the environment, you must conserve energy.*

In second conditional sentences we can use could, would, should, ought to and might + bare infinitive in the result clause.
*If we co-operated on the project, it might be more successful.*

In third conditional sentences we can use could, would, should, ought to, might and needn't + perfect infinitive.
*If you had asked a question, I might have answered.*

We can sometimes use modal verbs in the if clause.
*If I can do anything, let me know.*
*If we ought to have been there, they should have told us.*

**Circle the correct words.**

1  If I could / can travel round the world, I would.
2  If you'd thought of an idea, you should / needn't have suggested it.
3  They might / must save energy if they watch less TV.
4  If Jan can't / can convince them, nobody can.
5  If there's a problem, you must get / have got help.

# Writing task

*Imagine you are a member of your school's environmental group. You have been asked to write a report on a project your group is doing called* Conserving Energy. *Write a report informing teachers and students about what the group has done so far and what you plan to do in the future.*

## Write right!

**Use these steps to write your report.**

**Step 1**  Underline the parts in the Writing task that tell you what you have to do.

**Step 2**  Make a list of possible ways of conserving energy.

**Step 3**  Choose three ways to focus on and make notes on why they are necessary, what they involve and what benefits they offer. Do some research if necessary.

**Step 4**  Make a plan for your report and decide which way of conserving energy the group has already done some work on and which ones you'll recommend doing in the future. Use the plan opposite to help you.

**Step 5**  Use your notes, your plan and the useful language above to write your report.

**Step 6**  Edit your report when you have finished to check you have used linking words.

## Discussion

'The future of the planet is in our hands. It's up to us to protect it.' Discuss.

# 8 Technology

This may look like a work of art, but in fact it is a very sophisticated machine known as the Large Hadron Collider (LHC). It is located in a tunnel in Switzerland and its purpose is to cause minute particles to smash together at extremely high speeds. Scientists hope that the results they gain from the LHC will enable them to shed some light on some of the many mysteries that surround physics and the laws of nature. Although the LHC is in Switzerland, scientists from around the world worked together to build it and are studying the results together.

## Quiz

**How long is the tunnel in which the
Large Hadron Collider is housed?**

a  27 metres

b  27 kilometres

c  270 kilometres

# 8 Lesson 1

## Reading

**Read the report about e-waste. What are e-cycling centres?**

# E-waste – a global problem

E-waste is fast becoming a serious global problem. (1) _____

### The source of e-waste
We live in a society that constantly produces and consumes electronic products. It is often cheaper to buy new pieces of equipment than to repair old ones. Also, through clever advertising, companies persuade consumers to swap their old TVs, mobile phones and computers for the latest models. E-waste is created when we throw away electronic equipment like this. In the EU alone, about 8.7 million tonnes of e-waste is produced each year. (2) _____

### The problem with e-waste
Dumping e-waste in landfills or burning it causes serious problems for the environment. (3) _____ These substances can then leak into the ground in landfills or pollute the air when they are burnt.

### Global recycling schemes
(4) _____ However, their schemes are not always managed properly and sometimes electronics are just sent to developing countries such as Ghana. Here they are often burnt in public areas, which is very bad for people's health. Setting up recycling programmes in the countries that create e-waste could solve this problem. E-cycling centres could recycle the parts that we can reuse and properly dispose of the rest.

### Take-back policy
Another solution to e-waste is to make manufacturers responsible for their used products. This could mean forcing them to take back old products which are no longer wanted. (5) _____

### Consuming less
We can all reduce the amount of waste we produce by buying electrical products only when we have to. (6) _____

### Conclusion
E-waste is a serious issue in the modern world. Both manufacturers and consumers must accept their responsibilities and make an effort to keep it to a minimum.

## Comprehension

**Complete the report with these sentences.**

a In recent years, many countries have started recycling e-waste.

b They should then make sure they are properly recycled or reused.

c Sadly, just over one million tonnes is recycled.

d By resisting the temptation to buy a product just to have the latest version, we cut down on e-waste.

e This report will examine this problem and provide some possible solutions.

f Electronics contain dangerous chemicals and metals.

## Vocabulary

**Complete the sentences with these words.**

| dispose | leak | persuade | reuse | repair | swap |
| --- | --- | --- | --- | --- | --- |

1 Dangerous substances can _____ into the ground from batteries.

2 Let's try to _____ Dad to recycle plastic.

3 You should always _____ of electronic goods carefully.

4 I've decided to _____ my old laptop for a new one.

5 Don't throw away that bottle! _____ it!

6 My phone's broken. Can you _____ it?

# Grammar

## Gerunds and infinitives

We can use the gerund as the subject or object of a sentence; after prepositions; after the verb *go* to describe activities; after certain verbs and phrases (eg *avoid, be used to, can't help, consider, have difficulty, feel like, include, involve, it's no use, it's not worth, suggest*). After some verbs, an object can sometimes come between the verb and the gerund (*feel, hear, listen to, notice, see* and *watch*) to talk about an action in progress.
*Repairing things is better than throwing them away.*
*He was fined for dumping his computer on the street.*
*It's no use complaining about e-waste if you don't take action.*

We can use the full infinitive after certain verbs and phrases (eg *afford, allow, arrange, decide, expect, learn, make an effort, manage, offer, pretend, promise, refuse, seem*); after certain adjectives (eg *afraid, angry, anxious, glad, happy, nice, pleased, sad, sorry, stupid, surprised, upset*); and after *too* and *enough* + adjective. After some verbs, an object can sometimes come between the verb and the infinitive (eg *advise, choose, force, expect, tell, persuade*).
*I'm pleased to say the latest model is now available.*
*The problem of e-waste is too serious to ignore.*
*We must persuade companies to accept responsibility.*

We can use either the gerund or the full infinitive after certain verbs (*begin, continue, hate, intend, like, love, start*) without a change in meaning.
*I love sending text messages. = I love to send text messages.*

We can use either the gerund or the full infinitive after certain verbs (*forget, go on, mean, remember, stop, try*) but there is a change in meaning.
*I forgot to buy a CD. = I didn't buy a CD.*
*I forgot buying a CD. = I bought a CD, but I didn't remember doing it.*

**A Look back at the highlighted gerunds and infinitives in the report. Which:**

1 follows a preposition?
2 is the subject of the sentence?
3 follows a verb + object?
4 follows a certain phrase?
5 follows an adjective?

**B Complete the sentences with the gerund or the full infinitive formed from these verbs.**

> buy   lock   play   say   send   swim

1 I'm sorry _____ this technology isn't very effective.
2 Are you interested in _____ this device from me?
3 Fahd finds _____ with gadgets fascinating.
4 I noticed Jack _____ a text message in class.
5 My house was burgled because I forgot _____ the door.
6 I want to go _____ in the sea.

## Collocations

**Complete these phrases with hold or keep.**

1 _____ a secret
2 _____ an account of
3 _____ an opinion
4 _____ someone responsible for
5 _____ the line
6 _____ to a minimum
7 _____ your breath
8 _____ your word

# Speaking

**Ask and answer these questions with your partner.**

1 Do you own any gadgets? What do they do?
2 Are there any gadgets you would like? Why?
3 Are there any gadgets which you do not want? Why?

# Writing

**Write an advert for a gadget that you no longer need. Say what the product is, what condition it's in, why someone should buy it instead of a new one and how much you're selling it for.**

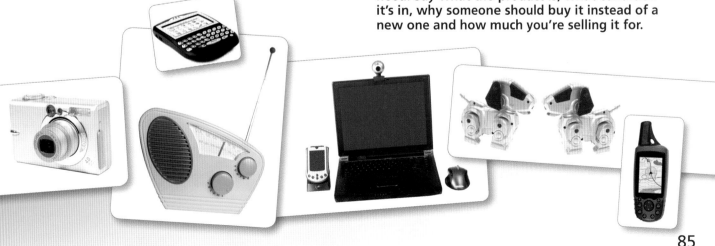

## Reading

Read the article to find out which invention is linked to a dog.

**Discussion**

'Our society depends on science and technology, yet hardly anyone knows anything about science and technology.' Discuss.

# Biomimetics *Technology that's as smart as nature*

Imagine a device that allows people to draw water from desert sands so that drought becomes a thing of the past. This may seem like science fiction, but thanks to biomimetics, it may become a reality. Biomimetics is the term we use to describe technology which imitates nature, and it is used in engineering, design and medicine.

Andrew Parker, a biologist, is inspired by biomimetics. His job is to study nature to see how we can learn from it. He discovered that the thorny devil lizard, which is found in the Australian desert, can 'drink' water through its foot. The water travels across its skin and up into its mouth. This makes it possible for it to get any water available from the desert sand. Parker and the engineers who work with him want to mimic the lizard's bizarre ability so that they can create a device to solve water shortages in areas of drought.

Another design that has used these principles is the Mercedes Bionic concept car, which is based on the boxfish. As its name suggests, the boxfish is shaped like a box. It is light but stable with skin that is very strong, and it cuts through water efficiently. In tests, the Mercedes Bionic has also proved to be very efficient, using around 20% less fuel than other cars of its size. It also mimics the boxfish's strength and stability. Although the Mercedes Bionic is not for sale, future Mercedes cars will have some of its features.

A less hi-tech example, but one which is extremely practical in our everyday lives, is Velcro. This clever fastener is used on clothes, shoes, to hold cables together and for many other purposes. Even a toddler can use it, yet it fastens very securely. Its hook and loop design was invented in the 1940s by Georges de Mestral who noticed how firmly prickly seeds stuck to his dog's coat. He imitated these two elements of nature in order to make Velcro, which soon became very popular throughout the world.

Of course, there are still many things which scientists who are involved in biomimetics can learn from nature. However, one of the biggest challenges they still face is to use their knowledge to create products that will make a profit.

## Comprehension

**Write A if the sentence is correct and B if it is not correct.**

1 A machine that takes water out of sand has been invented. ☐

2 Andrew Parker discovered the thorny devil lizard. ☐

3 The boxfish isn't a very good swimmer. ☐

4 You can't buy a Mercedes Bionic car. ☐

5 Velcro is easy to use. ☐

6 Scientists need to create products that can make money. ☐

**Guess what!**

A swimming costume which mimics sharks' skin has been developed in order to allow top athletes to swim faster.

# Vocabulary

**Find the words in the text and circle the correct meaning, a or b. The words are in the same order as they appear in the text.**

1 draw
   a take out
   b create a picture

2 inspired
   a brilliant
   b motivated

3 available
   a obtainable
   b vacant

4 principles
   a theories
   b opinions

5 stable
   a steady
   b balanced

6 efficient
   a well organised
   b without wasting fuel

7 firmly
   a securely
   b determinedly

8 coat
   a item of clothing
   b fur

# Grammar

## Clauses of purpose

We use clauses of purpose to explain the reason why someone does something or why something happens. We introduce them using these words and phrases: full infinitive; in order to + bare infinitive; so as to + bare infinitive; so that + subject and verb; in case + subject and verb; for + noun.

*We use technology to make our lives easier.*
*They studied birds so that they could find out how their wings worked.*
*He used a microscope in order to examine the fabric.*
*The scientists are looking to nature for ideas.*

**Circle the correct words.**

1 The lab was closed for / in case repairs.

2 They hired a new researcher to / for do the job.

3 He wants an MP3 player so as to / so that he can listen to music on the bus.

4 Ring the technician in order to / in case anything goes wrong.

5 Read the manual in order to / so as find out how to use the dishwasher.

6 Let's do some trials so as to / so that test the car's performance.

# Vocabulary

**Write the correct words.**

> cable    cash card    cash point
> memory stick    PIN    Velcro

_____

_____

_____

_____

_____

_____

# Listening

🎧 **Listen to the dialogue about wacky inventions and change the words in bold to make the sentences true.**

1 Grace is looking for ideas **in a catalogue**.      _____

2 Floppers have got **brushes** stuck to them.      _____

3 The slippers aren't **humorous** enough for Catherine.  _____

4 The personal cash point has its own **money box** and PIN.      _____

5 Catherine's got lots of **Inflators**.      _____

6 Grace's mum will pay for the cash point **in cash**.  _____

## Prepositions

**Complete the sentences with as or like.**

1 Brenda works _____ a computer analyst.

2 They built a device shaped _____ a fly.

3 The personal cash point looks _____ an ordinary cash point.

4 Most of her colleagues respect Jan _____ a scientist.

5 Andrew dressed up _____ a robot.

6 Mike's only the IT manager but he acts _____ it's his company.

## Vocabulary

**A** Write the correct words.

| binoculars | earphones | games console | home cinema | printer | USB cable |

1 _____
2 _____
3 _____
4 _____
5 _____
6 _____

**B** Match.

| 1 | GPS unit | a | ability to see |
| 2 | planetarium | b | device that detects light, sound or heat |
| 3 | sensor | c | new idea or method |
| 4 | vision | d | machine used for navigation |
| 5 | innovation | e | store of information on a computer |
| 6 | database | f | building or device with image of night sky |

## Listening skills

**A** Look at the questions and options in B. Talk to your partner about which options are likely answers and why.

**B** 🎧 Listen to part of a programme on technology and tick (✓) the correct box.

1 According to the speaker, a Personal Planetarium is
  a  a place where you can go to look at the stars. ☐
  b  a device which recognises stars and planets. ☐
  c  a programme which includes information about space. ☐

2 The device doesn't include
  a  TV programmes. ☐
  b  talks from experts. ☐
  c  facts and figures about space. ☐

3 You can use the USB cable to
  a  move information from your computer to the planetarium. ☐
  b  store data from the planetarium on your computer. ☐
  c  listen to talks on the planetarium. ☐

## Listening task

🎧 You will hear a speaker talking about night vision technology. For each question, tick (✓) the correct box.

1 The speaker says people may have seen night vision technology used
  a  by the police. ☐
  b  in films. ☐
  c  by the army. ☐

2 Night vision devices obtain light from
  a  the moon and stars only. ☐
  b  a special light on the device only. ☐
  c  all of the above. ☐

3 The human eye
  a  can see green more easily than other colours. ☐
  b  can only see one colour in the dark. ☐
  c  can't see the colour green at night. ☐

4 The speaker says the night vision devices are for
  a  everybody. ☐
  b  criminals. ☐
  c  soldiers. ☐

5 The Night Vision Binoculars cost
  a  £98. ☐
  b  £172. ☐
  c  £1,000. ☐

## Listen Up!

🎧 **Listen to Simon and Ella doing this speaking task and answer the questions.**

*The leader of your local youth club must decide which piece of new equipment to buy for the club. Work with a partner to talk about the suggestions in the pictures and decide which two are most appropriate for all the members of the club.*

1 Which items do the speakers chose?

2 What reasons do they give to support their choices?

3 Do they completely agree on all points?

4 Why do they reject the other alternatives?

5 Do you agree with their choices?

6 Do they discuss all the alternatives?

## Speaking skills

A Look at this list of appliances which could also have been in the Speaking task you heard in *Listen Up!*. Put a tick (✓) next to the ones you think are good ideas for the youth club and a cross (✗) next to the ones you think are bad ideas.

| | | | |
|---|---|---|---|
| digital camera | ☐ | microwave oven | ☐ |
| DVD player | ☐ | music centre | ☐ |
| electric piano | ☐ | printer | ☐ |

B Now complete these sentences using your own words to talk about the suggestions in A.

1 If it was up to me, I'd …

2 My advice would be to …

3 If I was in the leader's shoes, I'd …

4 The youth club leader would be better …

5 He should …

6 Why don't we suggest …?

## Speaking tasks

A Read the Speaking task in B and look at the pictures. Decide which ideas below could be used to talk about the items shown in the pictures.

> a creative way to spend time
> dangers of the Internet
> benefits of computers
> easy to use
> entertaining hobby
> risk of becoming addicted
> negative effects on behaviour
> expensive
> a waste of time
> educational

B A friend of yours is giving a talk on modern technology in young people's lives and has asked you to help him decide what to talk about. Work with a partner and talk about the subjects in the pictures and decide which two are most appropriate.

## Linking words and phrases 2

> We can use linking words and phrases to show how a sentence or paragraph relates to the previous one. For example, we can use them to add information, to order information, to show a result, and to show contrast.

**Write A (adds information), O (orders information), R (shows result), or C (shows contrast).**

1  as a result ☐
2  consequently ☐
3  despite ☐
4  finally ☐
5  first of all ☐
6  however ☐
7  in addition ☐
8  moreover ☐
9  on the other hand ☐
10  secondly ☐
11  therefore ☐
12  this means that ☐

## Writing task

**A  Read the Writing task and tick (✓) the things the writer will complain about.**

1  late delivery ☐
2  take-back policy ineffective ☐
3  zoom lens not working ☐
4  doesn't stay charged for 60 hours ☐
5  smaller screen than advertised ☐
6  faulty scene selector ☐
7  too heavy ☐
8  cost ☐

*You recently bought a digital camcorder online after seeing the advert below for it. However, there are several problems with the camera and you want a replacement. Use your notes on the advert to write an email complaining about it.*

*still waiting for my old one to be picked up*

*needs recharging after an hour's use*

**Supersonic Digital Camcorder**

Free delivery within 5 working days and we take back and recycle your old model

**Camcorder features:**
- X 70 zoom lens
- up to 60 hours recording time
- 2.5 inch LCD screen  ← *doesn't work*
- intelligent scene selector
- photo facility
- weight 290 grams

Was £349.99, now £299.99, save £50  ← *I paid old price.*

**B  Complete the model email with the linking words. Why has each one been used?**

 Consequently    First of all     However    In addition    To conclude

*model composition*

---

**Email**

New   Reply   Forward   Print   Delete

Dear Sir/Madam,

I am writing to complain about a camcorder I purchased from your website. I am extremely unhappy with the product and your company's services.

(1) _____, the advert claims the camcorder can record for up to sixty hours. (2) _____, the product I received must be recharged every hour. Moreover, I chose this model because of its intelligent scene selector feature. Unfortunately, it does not work on my camcorder. I had it checked by a professional photographer and she confirmed a fault.

Furthermore, I am disappointed with the company's services. I was charged the old price quoted in the advert, and by the time I realised, it was too late, so I paid £50 more than I should have. (3) _____, I called the helpline to ask for a refund. I was told to choose another product priced £50 or more. I believe this is highly unacceptable as it was not my mistake.

The final point I wish to make is about the promise to take back and recycle old models. The man who delivered my new camcorder refused to take away the old one. I later made arrangements to have my old camcorder picked up, but nobody appeared.

(4) _____, I expect a new camcorder and a £50 refund. (5) _____, you should not say that you take back and recycle old products unless you ensure that the service works.

Yours faithfully,

Marsha Hunt

# Analyse it!

Write T (true) or F (false) to say what the writer of the model email does.

1 complains about all points she noted on the advert ☐
2 complains about other features of the product ☐
3 says how the problems should be dealt with ☐
4 uses the exact wording used in his/her notes ☐
5 writes with a firm but polite tone ☐
6 uses formal language ☐
7 orders points logically ☐

# Writing plan

Complete the plan for the model email with these sentences.

a Discuss a problem with service received.
b Discuss another problem with service received.
c Discuss the problems with the product.
d State the reason for writing.
e State what action you expect the reader to take.

Paragraph 1 _____
Paragraph 2 _____
Paragraph 3 _____
Paragraph 4 _____
Paragraph 5 _____

# Grammar

## Causative form

We use the causative form to talk about something:
a that someone does for us.
   *Ralf will have the dishwasher repaired tomorrow.*
b bad that happened to us which we didn't want to happen.
   *Clare has had her laptop stolen.*

We make the causative form using have + an object + the past participle of the main verb. The verb have can be used in any tense and come after a modal verb. The object of a causative sentence must appear before the past participle.
*She has had her phone cut off again!*
*They must have their TV fixed.*

> **Note:** In informal English, we can use get instead of have to talk about something we ask someone to do for us. However, we must use have when we use causative form to talk about something bad that happened to us.
> *I'm getting my new computer delivered at 9 o'clock.*

## Write sentences with the causative form.

1 we / get / our leaflets / print / tonight
2 Fran / have / her webcam / damage / yesterday
3 we / will / have / our cables / repair / tomorrow
4 I / think / you / should / have / your mobile phone / fix
5 they / always / get / photos / develop / at Digiprint

# useful language

## Complaining

I am writing to complain about …
I am extremely disappointed with …
I believe this is utterly unacceptable as/because …
I feel I am owed/should receive …
I expect + noun/you + full infinitive …
I insist on + noun/you + full infinitive …

# Writing task

*You bought a printer online after seeing the advert below for it. However, there are several problems with the printer and you want a replacement. Use your notes on the advert to write an email complaining about it.*

*Print your own photos easily and cheaply with the Sonsson full colour printer!*

**Printer features:**

- printing speeds – up to 21 colour pages per minute and colour photos in 18 seconds ← *took me 10 minutes*
- easy printing directly from Internet — *no it doesn't*
- prints directly from camera using USB cable
- holds 125 sheets of paper — *I didn't get this.*

Free ink with every order! ← *Found it for £99.99, but didn't get refund!*

Buy now for £125 – if you find it cheaper anywhere else, we'll refund the difference!

# Write right!

**Use these steps to help you write your email.**

**Step 1** Look at the notes in the Writing task and the points they are related to. Group similar points together and decide on the order they will appear in.

**Step 2** Decide how you could reword them to make them more formal.

**Step 3** Make a plan for your email. Include a paragraph saying why you're writing, 2 or 3 complaints paragraphs and a paragraph saying what action should be taken. Use the plan opposite to help you.

**Step 4** Use the notes, your plan and the useful language above to write your email. Make sure you use linking words and phrases properly.

## Discussion

'Technology isn't dangerous. It's how it's used that can do harm.' Discuss.

# Review 4

## Vocabulary

### A Circle the correct words.

1 Can you tilt / repair the computer screen up a bit?

2 This method involves the emission / conversion of sunlight into energy.

3 We're visiting the home cinema / planetarium this weekend.

4 Is your knowledge of history up to source / scratch?

5 There has been a water explosion / shortage in our town lately.

6 He kept his memory / word and started recycling his waste.

7 I'll hold / keep you responsible for recycling.

8 How much information is on the database / dam?

### B Complete the paragraph with these words.

face up to   keep   leak
pollute   stop   turn to

## What's the solution?

Most people are aware that the environment is in danger, but few people really (1) _____ the situation. The truth is that the Earth's temperature is rising and the polar ice caps are melting. If this is allowed to continue, some countries may find themselves under water. Governments and individuals must act now to prevent this from happening. One solution could be to severely punish companies that (2) _____ the atmosphere or rivers when dangerous substances (3) _____ from their factories into the water. Some companies will (4) _____ at nothing to make a profit and this is why governments must take action immediately. As for individuals, we must understand how we pollute the Earth every day and (5) _____ greener alternatives where possible. For example, we can walk or cycle instead of taking the car. Most cars use fossil fuels which pollute the environment. It's essential, therefore, to (6) _____ their use to a minimum and find practical ways to reduce our energy consumption.

### C Write the correct words.

cell   coat   drought
GPS unit   landfill   panel

_____

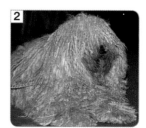

_____

_____

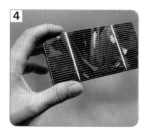

_____

_____

_____

## Grammar

### A Choose the correct answers.

1 If water reaches 0°, it _____ .
a  will freeze          b  freezes          c  would freeze

2 It's no use _____ e-cycling centres if nobody uses them.
a  setting up          b  to set up          c  set up

3 He went to a talk _____ to find out about GPS technology.
a  in order          b  so that          c  for

4 If only I _____ a home cinema!
a  would afford     b  could afford     c  should afford

5 Karim _____ his cash card taken away.
a  got          b  had          c  was

6 Wayne wishes he _____ his old TV for a new one.
a  swaps          b  would swap          c  had swapped

**B** Look at the picture and complete the sentences with the correct form of these words.

> convert   install   not fill   save   see

1 Mr and Mrs Jenkins are having photovoltaic panels _____ at the moment.

2 If the recycling bin _____ with plants, they could recycle their rubbish.

3 They have put on all the lights so as _____ better.

4 If they closed the windows and front door, they _____ energy.

5 If only they _____ to a renewable energy source sooner, they would have polluted the environment less.

**C** Circle the correct words.

1 If you use solar power, you **will / wouldn't** save money.

2 Why don't you suggest **to save / saving** paper at school?

3 Call our Helpline if you **had / have** any questions.

4 There **is / will be** a drought if it doesn't rain soon.

5 I wish my electricity bill **wasn't / isn't** so high.

6 If I had £600 I **would buy / had bought** that gadget.

**D** The words in bold are wrong. Write the correct words.

1 I wish this laptop **isn't** so expensive.        _____

2 Oh no! Sonia's **got** her mobile phone stolen!        _____

3 She wrote down her PIN **in order** as to remember it.        _____

4 If only you **haven't** deleted the database!        _____

5 Did you mean **switching** off the electricity or was it an accident?        _____

6 If a DVD player **was** faulty, the company gives a refund.        _____

## Quiz time!

Are you a techno kid or an environment freak? Find out with this quick quiz.

1 How do you travel to school?
   a   by public transport or school bus
   b   by bike or on foot
   c   by car or moped

2 Which of the following would you most like your school to have?
   a   a personal planetarium
   b   fields for growing fruit and vegetables in
   c   laptops for each student in your class

3 Which possession couldn't you live without?
   a   your electric guitar
   b   your favourite board game
   c   the latest games console and video games

4 What would you rather do on a Saturday morning?
   a   go shopping with friends
   b   clean up a nearby beach or forest
   c   watch TV

5 What is your attitude towards environmental pollution?
   a   It's a huge problem, but there's not a lot I can do about it.
   b   It's terrible and we are all responsible for saving the planet.
   c   I don't know because I haven't played that video game yet.

6 What is your opinion of modern technology?
   a   It's great, but we should only use it when we need it.
   b   It has only got negative effects on our lives.
   c   It's extremely important in our lives today.

**Check your answers and read your analysis.**

**Have you scored mainly a's?**
You are middle of the road. This means that you are aware that the Earth is in danger, but you're not quite sure how you can help. Don't worry because some of your lifestyle choices help to reduce damage to the environment, but you might just not have realised it. As for technology, you recognise its benefits and use it to your advantage. You also know that there are some dangers involved in using modern technology too much and are cautious about it.

**Have you scored mainly b's?**
You really are an earth kid! You are very concerned about the destruction of our environment and will stop at nothing to put things right. Your whole lifestyle is built around activities that involve conservation in some way. You are not a fan of modern technology at all and believe that it can only do us harm.

**Have you scored mainly c's?**
You are undoubtedly a techno kid! Technological devices are the most important thing in your life. You believe that electronic appliances make your life more entertaining and easier. You don't think much about the negative effects of technology. You believe that adults should be the ones to sort out problems of any kind.

In an age when nearly everything is produced in factories, it is very unusual to find a traditional industry that is still successful. An example of such an industry, however, can be found here at the tanneries of Fes, Morocco. The men who work here make leather out of animal hides using various natural substances to treat and dye the material. They use the same methods that have been used for centuries, and the leather they produce is considered to be of the highest quality. When it is finished, leather workers who work nearby use the material to make traditional goods such as babouches (slippers) and poufs (cushions) as well as bags and jackets.

**Quiz**

**Which of the following sectors do 40-45% of the population of Morocco work in?**

a  agriculture

b  the textile industry

c  tourism

**Discussion**

'Work is good for you.' Discuss.

## Reading

**Read Dan's email. What have Dan and Julie agreed?**

---

Email

New | Reply | Forward | Print | Delete

---

Hi Uma,

How are you? I hope you've all settled into your new house and neighbourhood. It must be a big change for you all. Did you use the removals company Dad suggested in the end?

There has been a big change in my family too. Unfortunately, it isn't a good one. Basically, Dad was made redundant from his job as an estate agent just after you left and he's still unemployed. As you can imagine, this is putting a lot of strain on us all because we don't know when he'll find another job because of the recession. Very few companies are taking on new staff at the moment.

Dad's been for two interviews at estate agencies but he hasn't been successful. He's quite worried about the situation as he says that employers probably think he's too old to take on. I told him this is crazy because he's only forty two. He's also concerned that we might not be able to keep up with the mortgage payments on our house unless he finds something soon.

Luckily, Mum can still look on the bright side. She says something will turn up sooner or later and that we can all economise until it does. She's also asked her boss to give her overtime whenever possible to increase her income. My sister Julie and I have agreed not to ask for pocket money or treats so that we can cut down on spending. I have also applied for a Saturday job at a local shoe shop. I'll let you know if I get it.

Mum's very supportive of Dad and helps him a great deal with job-hunting. Last night she told him he should maybe consider retraining in a field that hasn't been affected by the recession. She said he could easily become an accounts teacher since he's got a degree in accounting, and schools are always looking for staff. So he's considering doing a teacher-training course in the autumn. He might even be able to get a grant to do it. Mum says he's practically guaranteed a job once he graduates.

That's all for now. I'll keep you informed of any changes.

Take care,

Dan

---

## Comprehension

**The words in bold are wrong. Write the correct words.**

1  Dan's dad used to work **for a removals company**.  _____

2  **A lot of** companies are taking on new employees now.  _____

3  Dan's dad feels **happy** about his situation.  _____

4  Dan's mum wants to work **fewer hours**.  _____

5  **Julie** is trying to get a Saturday job.  _____

6  Dan's dad might **start teaching** in the autumn.  _____

# Vocabulary

**Circle the correct words.**

1 The company is making / putting 12,000 people redundant.

2 Gayle wants to retrain / take on as a nurse.

3 Estate agents / Removals companies help people move house.

4 Some employees don't get paid for job-hunting / overtime.

5 Mark has been given a grant / mortgage to study at college.

6 Our income / recession has dropped by 30 percent this year.

# Grammar

## Reported Speech 1: Statements

We use reported speech to tell someone what another person has said. When we use reported speech, we change the verb tense to a tense further back in the past. We also change personal pronouns (I, you, etc), possessive adjectives (my, your, etc), possessive pronouns (mine, yours, etc) if they're used to talk about the original speaker, and demonstrative pronouns (this, these).

The most common verbs we use with reported speech are say and tell. When we use tell with reported speech it is followed by an object.

*'Mandy wants to be the head of finance,' he said.*
*He said (that) Mandy wanted to be the head of finance.*

*'We're looking for an assistant,' she said.*
*She said (that) they were looking for an assistant.*

*'He was sacked from his last job,' I said.*
*I said (that) he had been sacked from his last job.*

*'They'll be working on my project,' Diana told me.*
*Diana told me (that) they would be working on her project.*

*'I must finish this report,' she told the employee.*
*She told the employee (that) she had to finish that report.*

> **Note:** We do not change present tenses when we are talking about what still exists. There is also no tense change with the following: Past Perfect Simple, Past Perfect Continuous, second and third conditional sentences, would, could, might, should, ought to, used to, had better, mustn't and must when it is used to express deduction.
> *'The new member of staff is great,' he said.*
> *He said (that) the new member of staff is great.*

## Changes in time and place

When we use reported speech, words and phrases that talk about time and place usually change.
*'I'm working with Jim tomorrow,' said Jo.*
*Jo said (that) she was working with Jim the next/following day.*

*'They missed the meeting yesterday,' Jake said.*
*Jake said (that) they had missed the meeting the day before.*

*'They're too busy to help you at the moment,' she said.*
*She said (that) they were too busy to help us at that moment.*

*'You can leave your tools here,' I told the plumber.*
*I told the plumber (that) he could leave his tools there.*

**A Write these sentences in reported speech. Sometimes more than one answer is possible.**

1 'The manager wants to see you,' Darren told me.

2 'Elizabeth is training to be an accountant,' said Eddie.

3 'I can't do overtime this weekend,' Sarah said.

4 'You have been at your desk since yesterday,' he said.

5 'Ian ought to explain things more clearly,' said Mary.

**B Read the sentences and write what the people said. Sometimes more than one answer is possible.**

1 He said he'd been working since the year before.

2 The electrician said he would be back the next day.

3 Amanda said she had sent the emails on time.

4 Maged told me he wouldn't be coming to the party.

5 The trainer told me I should pass the course.

## Word formation

**Complete the sets of sentences with the correct word. Which part of speech is each word?**

1 **economics    economise    economist**

   a People who are unemployed must try to
   _____ .

   b Billy studied _____ at university.

   c An _____ studies financial markets.

2 **graduate    graduate    graduation**

   a Clark is a _____ of Yale University.

   b Jo's _____ ceremony is next week.

   c When will you _____ from college?

3 **applicant    application    apply**

   a She's the best _____ for the job.

   b You should _____ for this job.

   c He's sent six letters of _____ today.

4 **embarrass    embarrassed    embarrassment**

   a Sam felt _____ about her mistake.

   b Please don't _____ yourself.

   c What an _____ ! I can't believe she heard us arguing!

# Speaking

**Work with a partner. Take it in turns to tell each other about the career you want. Talk about what is involved, why you like it as well as the qualifications and experience you need. Make notes about what your partner said.**

# Writing

**Write a paragraph about what your partner said in the Speaking task. Use your notes and reported speech.**

**Discussion**

'In some jobs it's necessary to take risks.' Discuss.

## Reading

**Read the article about a researcher called Sylvia Earle. What was a Tektite Habitat?**

# It's research, but not as we know it

If the word *researcher* brings to mind someone who works in a laboratory doing experiments or reads all day in a library, then meet Dr Sylvia Earle. Dr Earle has carried out much of her research deep under the sea. Her outstanding work at sea has included leading around 70 expeditions and spending over 6,500 hours under the water. She also holds the world record for the deepest solo walk on the ocean floor at a depth of 381 metres. It's no wonder she has been given the nickname 'Her Deepness.'

As a child, Dr Earle was always interested in wildlife and was never afraid to investigate nature. Her parents told her to touch animals and insects, and not to be afraid of them. When she was older, she was given the opportunity to develop this interest thanks to scholarships to study botany at university. She also enrolled on courses in scuba diving and decided to devote herself to marine biology. It was this decision and her determined character that led her to have a truly remarkable career.

After several years of diving, Dr Earle asked if she could take part in a research expedition in an underwater laboratory. The laboratory was called a Tektite Habitat and it allowed divers to remain under the water to carry out research for weeks at a time. In 1970 an all-female group went on the sixth mission of the Tektite II scientists-in-the-sea programme. Dr Earle was asked if she would lead that mission. Along with another four women – three scientists and an engineer – she stayed in the Tektite Habitat for two weeks. During this time, Dr Earle and the other scientists gathered and analysed data on marine life.

Marine life has always been at the centre of Dr Earle's work and she is highly respected for her expertise in this field. She is often asked to give talks by environmental groups about marine life as well as her plan to create a global network of marine protected areas. What makes her extra special is that she doesn't look upon her work as a job, but as her vocation in life.

## Comprehension

**Answer the questions.**

1  How far below sea level did Dr Earle walk when she set the world record?

2  What did Dr Earle's parents encourage her to do?

3  What did funding enable Dr Earle to do when she was a young woman?

4  How many people in total went on the Tektite II mission Dr Earle led?

5  What did the team in the Tektite Habitat do?

6  What does Dr Earle hope to achieve in the future?

**Guess what!**

The Challenger Deep, in the southern part of the Mariana Trench in the Western Pacific, is the deepest point of the ocean at approximately 11,000 metres beneath sea level.

# Vocabulary

**Find words in the article that have these meanings. The words are in the same order as they appear in the text.**

1  excellent _____
2  a funny name that is not a person's real name _____
3  sums of money given to help pay for education _____
4  give most of your attention to something _____
5  knowledge of a particular subject _____
6  a job or way of life suited to someone _____

# Grammar

## Reported speech 2: Questions, Commands and Requests

### Questions
We usually use the verb ask to report questions. The changes that we make in reported statements are also made in reported questions.
When a question begins with a question word, we use that word to form the reported question.
*'Who made this mistake?' the supervisor asked.*
*The supervisor asked who had made that mistake.*

When a question hasn't got a question word, we use if or whether in the reported question.
*'Are you taking next week off?' Carol asked.*
*Carol asked if/whether I was taking the following week off.*

### Commands
We usually use the verb tell to report commands. Tell is followed by an object and the full infinitive. When the command is negative, we put not before the full infinitive.
*'Don't accept any more bookings!' the manager said.*
*The manager told me not to accept any more bookings.*

### Requests
We usually use the verb ask to report requests. We form reported requests in the same way as reported commands. We miss out the word please in reported requests.
*'Please be at the construction site by 7.30,' Stan said.*
*Stan asked us to be at the construction site by 7.30.*

**A  Tick (✓) the second sentences in each pair if they are correct and correct the ones that are wrong.**

1  'What is the salary?' he asked.
   He asked what the salary is.
2  'We're making you redundant, John,' they said.
   They told they were making him redundant.
3  'Don't write the article,' she said.
   She didn't tell me to write the article.
4  'How far did the divers go?' he asked.
   He asked me if the divers went far.
5  'Where did I leave my notes?' she asked.
   She asked me where she had left her notes.

---

**B  Look at the parts of the text that have been highlighted. What might have been said in each case?**

# Vocabulary

**Match.**

1  Her hat brings to           a  the ropes.
2  There are no current        b  dangerous conditions.
3  The boss showed me          c  free to ask questions.
4  I've enrolled on a          d  mind my mother.
5  Please feel                 e  cookery course.
6  Builders often work in      f  vacancies unfortunately.

# Listening

🎧 **Listen and circle the correct words.**

1  Patrick Thornton is a careers advisor / engineer / driver.
2  Patrick's new book is called *Job Alert* / *Test-drive Your Future Career* / *Which way now?*.
3  The new book doesn't include information on qualifications / working conditions / current vacancies.
4  If you want to try out a job you contact the presenter / Patrick / a mentor.
5  A test-drive lasts for up to two days / a week / six months.
6  The book has sold 1,500 / 2,000 / 6,000 copies so far.

## Phrasal Verbs

**Complete the sentences with the correct form of these phrasal verbs.**

> come along   cut out   get into
> look upon   put together

1  Sam isn't really _____ to be a lawyer.
2  We _____ a list of all vacancies and posted it on the web.
3  Why don't you _____ on our visit to the warehouse?
4  I can't believe I _____ university!
5  He always _____ his job as enjoyable.

## Vocabulary

**A  Write the correct words.**

> bricklayer    carpenter    civil engineer
> electrician    fork-lift truck driver    plumber

**B  Look at the list of equipment below. Which of these can you see in the pictures in A? Which ones do you think are necessary for each of the jobs in A?**

| | | | |
|---|---|---|---|
| 1 | protective gloves | 6 | spirit level |
| 2 | hard hat | 7 | drill |
| 3 | overalls | 8 | blueprints |
| 4 | goggles | 9 | tool belt |
| 5 | steel toe-capped boots | 10 | tool box |

## Listening skills

**A  Look at the sentences in B and underline adverbs of frequency, phrases that show sequence, comparatives and negative forms of verbs.**

**B  🎧 Listen to these short dialogues and tick (✓) the sentences that are true.**

1  At first, the girl thought her job didn't pay well. ☐

2  Bells and Hunter always replace workers that leave immediately. ☐

3  The boy thinks Jordan often looks a mess. ☐

4  Thomas thinks he should have been paid more. ☐

## Listening task

🎧 **Listen to Mrs Beattie and Michael talking on Michael's first day at work. Decide whether each statement is right (A) or wrong (B).**

| | | A | B |
|---|---|---|---|
| 1 | Mrs Beattie shows Michael what to do immediately. | ☐ | ☐ |
| 2 | It isn't the first time Michael has worn safety equipment. | ☐ | ☐ |
| 3 | Fork-lift truck drivers have the easiest jobs. | ☐ | ☐ |
| 4 | At first, Michael says he did his work experience the previous year. | ☐ | ☐ |
| 5 | Michael will only deal with boxes on the ground every day. | ☐ | ☐ |
| 6 | Mrs Beattie asks Michael to move the boxes on his own. | ☐ | ☐ |

## Talking about work

They're on a construction site/in an office/a classroom/ a warehouse/a factory.

The working conditions are dangerous/extremely difficult/excellent/fairly good.

He's/She's wearing protective clothing/a uniform/casual clothes/a suit.

He's/She's in charge of …

He/She works with his/her hands.

It's a highly-skilled /low-skilled job.

## Job titles

apprentice
manager
manual worker
supervisor
trainee
trainer

**B** Work with a partner to describe these pictures and discuss the people's working conditions.

# Listen Up!

🎧 Listen to Sakis and Eleni talking about these pictures in their classroom. Which words and phrases from *Express Yourself!* does each student use?

# Speaking skills

**A** Look at the pictures in B and make notes about the following.

- what job the people are doing
- where they are working
- what dangers they face
- what they are wearing and why
- what skills they need to do their job
- how important it is to get on with their colleagues

# Speaking tasks

**A** Look at the pictures in B and brainstorm as many words and expressions as you can think of related to them. Then put them into two columns with the headings *Working conditions* and *Relationships*.

**B** Work with a partner and take it in turns to describe the working conditions shown in these pictures and say what relationship the people might have. Student A should talk about picture 1 and Student B should talk about picture 2.

**C** Do any of the jobs in the pictures appeal to you? Why/Why not?

101

## Writing successful stories

> A successful short story must have 2-3 characters, an interesting plot and a clear beginning, middle and end. Good writers use several means to capture readers' interest and make them continue reading. These include using dramatic opening sentences; descriptive adjectives and adverbs; direct speech; short, dramatic sentences and sometimes a twist in the plot in which something unexpected happens.

**A  Write B for beginning, M for middle or E for end.**

1  Looking back, Mark realised how stupid he'd been to listen to his colleague. He promised himself that he'd never be so trusting again. ☐

2  It was the chance of a lifetime for Mark. He'd just been hired as a lawyer in one of the most successful companies in the country and he was determined to be a success. ☐

3  While he was preparing for court one day, a colleague paid him a visit. He seemed very anxious as he sat on Mark's desk and whispered 'Er... , Mark, I need your help with something.' ☐

**B  Look at these examples of language from a story and tick (✓) the lines which are best.**

1  Helen stopped and looked up, but then she couldn't move. ☐
   Helen froze. ☐

2  The robber raised his gun and screamed 'Lie on the floor!' ☐
   The robber raised his gun and told us to lie on the floor. ☐

3  The chair fell on the floor. ☐
   The chair spun round and clattered noisily to the floor. ☐

4  The manager glanced in the direction of the robber and stammered his reply. ☐
   The manager looked at the robber and then replied. ☐

## Writing task

**A  Read the writing task below and look at the picture. What do you think the story will be about?**
*Write a story with the title* Henry's last day.

**B  Read the model story and number the paragraphs in the correct order. Then underline examples of descriptive adjectives and adverbs, direct speech and short, dramatic sentences.**

*model composition*

# Henry's last day

☐ The following Friday, Luke arrived early, so he was shocked to see that the shop door was slightly open. He went inside nervously and saw the back of a tall man behind the counter. He was taking money out of the till and putting it into his wallet. Suddenly, the man swung round. It was Henry. 'Wh-What are you doing?' Luke stammered. 'Keep your mouth shut or you'll regret it!' said Henry, nastily.

☐ Luke was very excited on his first day at Quigley's Toy Shop. Mr Quigley welcomed him warmly, saying in his strong Scottish accent 'I'm sure you'll fit in nicely, Luke,' and Luke smiled back at him eagerly.

☐ At ten o'clock exactly a tall thin man entered. 'Ah, Henry!' said Mr Quigley. 'This is Luke, the new assistant.' 'Hello,' said Henry, coldly. Luke smiled but couldn't help feeling disappointed. Henry didn't seem to be as friendly as Mr Quigley had promised.

☐ A short time later, as Mr Quigley was informing Luke about the shop, he explained that he only worked on Fridays, and that the shop was usually run by the manager, Henry. He said that Henry was a good friend, and he promised to introduce him to Luke when he arrived at ten o'clock. 'You'll really like him!' he said.

☐ Just then Luke heard a familiar voice behind him. 'I saw everything, Henry,' said Mr Quigley, shaking. 'And I know you threatened Luke. Put that wallet down and get out of my shop!' Henry didn't need to be asked twice. He dropped the wallet and ran for the door without a backward glance.

# Analyse it!

**Answer the questions.**

1. How does Luke feel on his first day?
2. What does Henry look like?
3. Why is Luke disappointed?
4. What does Henry do behind the counter?
5. What kind of character do you think Mr Quigley has got?

# Writing plan

**Write the correct paragraph number from the model next to these descriptions.**

1. Describe the main event and the characters' reactions to it. ☐
2. Introduce a twist in the story and develop the characters. ☐
3. Bring the story to an end. ☐
4. Set the scene and introduce some of the main characters. ☐
5. Give background details about the situation leading up to the main event and introduce another character. ☐

# Grammar

## Reporting verbs

The most common reporting verbs are say and tell for statements, tell for commands and ask for questions and requests. However, there are other reporting verbs that we can use to report what the person said more accurately. Reporting verbs can be followed by a full infinitive (agree, offer, promise, refuse, threaten); by an object + full infinitive (advise, beg, command, invite, order, persuade, remind, warn), by a gerund (deny, suggest) by a preposition + a gerund (admit to, accuse somebody of, apologise for, boast about) or by that (announce, complain, deny, explain, exclaim, promise, protest, suggest).

*'I won't give you a pay rise,' the boss said.*
*The boss refused to give me a pay rise.*

*'Remember to put all the equipment in the cupboard,' she said.*
*She reminded us to put all the equipment in the cupboard.*

*'I didn't speak rudely to the customer,' the cashier said.*
*The cashier denied speaking rudely to the customer.*

*'You've been late twice this week,' the boss said.*
*The boss complained that I'd been late twice that week.*

**Rewrite these sentences using reported speech. Use these verbs.**

| accuse of | admit | deny | promise | refuse | suggest |
|---|---|---|---|---|---|

1. 'That customer stole some socks!' said the manager.
2. 'I won't do any more overtime,' Philip said.
3. 'We didn't work without our hard hats,' said the workers.
4. 'We'll increase your salary if you do this project,' they said.
5. 'Let's check these figures once again,' the accountant said.
6. 'I spilt hot soup down the lady's back,' the waiter said.

## useful language

**Ordering events**
It was the chance of a lifetime …
… had just got his/her big break.
At first, …
In the beginning, …
Just then, …
A few days/weeks/months later, …
After a while …
Looking back, …
At the end of the day, …

# Writing task

*Write a story with the title* My worst day at the office.

## Write right!

**Use these steps to help you write your story.**

**Step 1** Decide on 2-3 main characters and think about their appearances and personalities. Think of some adjectives that describe these characters.

**Step 2** Think about how the story will start and how events will develop. Then decide how the story will end.

**Step 3** Make a plan for your story and decide how you will organise the events. Use the plan above to help you.

**Step 4** Use your notes, your plan and the useful language above to write your story. Make sure you use a good opening sentence, plenty of adjectives and adverbs and both direct and reported speech.

**Step 5** Read your story carefully when you have finished to check that it has a beginning, a middle and an end, and that it is interesting to read.

## Discussion

What does being successful mean? Discuss this question in relation to the following:
a  earning a lot of money.
b  doing a job where you help others.

This helicopter is a special type of aircraft known as a helitanker. It is effective in fighting fires that cannot be reached by road vehicles. The helitanker takes water from nearby sources such as lakes or rivers, drawing it in with a large hose. The aircraft is then flown over the flames and anything from 1,000 to 10,000 litres of water is dropped from its tank. For hard-to-reach forest fires, aircraft such as the helitanker are the only means by which they can be tackled.

**What do people call the bucket that helicopters sometimes use to carry water?**

a   the Bambi bucket

b   the Mickey bucket

c   the Dumbo bucket

**Discussion**

'We should never waste firefighters' time.' Discuss.

## Reading

Read the firefighters' weekly log. What do you think would have made the firefighters angry?

### Monday 13th April

A call was received at 10.06 about a blaze in a warehouse on Townsend Quay. Two fire engines from Redding Fire Station were sent immediately. The firefighters found a well developed fire and Commander Eileen Millar quickly ordered the firefighters to use their breathing apparatus and then called for a third fire engine to be sent. The fire was tackled using jets and was fully extinguished within twenty five minutes. An investigation into the cause of the fire is now being conducted by Redding Fire Service.

### Wednesday 15th April

At 12.00, a road crash rescue exercise took place on the town's ring road. Firefighters from Waterfront, Grange, Redding and Castleton Fire Stations participated. Firefighters were given the task of rescuing passengers from the wrecks of two cars that had collided with each other. They used cutting equipment to free the passengers, who were actually firefighters from Grange Fire Station. Paramedics were also at the scene to provide medical assistance and Bracken Regional Police were put in charge of traffic management. Chief Commissionaire Jones later said 'The increasing number of road accidents in our region means it is essential that firefighters are trained in dealing with them. Today's firefighters showed they are more than capable of responding quickly to a 999 call and removing casualties safely from the scene of an accident.'

### Thursday 16th April

Several calls were received at 21.45 about a blaze at a school on Brighton Road. Two fire engines from Grange Fire Station were sent immediately and two from Castleton were put on stand-by. On arrival, firefighters found that it was in fact a hoax and that no fire had been started. The silly trick was played by an organised group since the calls were made from phone boxes in different neighbourhoods. To tackle this problem, it has been decided to make hoaxes one of the issues at Saturday's Fire Service Festival.

### Saturday 18th April

The Fire Service Festival took place in Castleton. The festival was aimed at informing the general public about everyday fire hazards. This

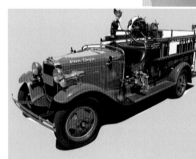

included demonstrations of how to extinguish frying pan fires as they are one of the most common causes of fires in the home. There was also a display of fire engines ranging from a vintage engine with hand-held pump to the very latest aerial rescue pump. The Grange Station drama group also put on a play about a shop that burns to the ground while firefighters are busy answering a false alarm.

## Comprehension

Write **M** (Monday), **W** (Wednesday), **T** (Thursday) and **S** (Saturday). On which day(s):

1  was there a real emergency?  ☐

2  did firefighters answer a false alarm?  ☐

3  did non-firefighters attend a special event?  ☐

4  were fires put out?  ☐ ☐

5  were fire vehicles on show?  ☐

6  was there a training exercise?  ☐

# Vocabulary

**Find words or phrases in the log which mean the same as the words in bold. The words and phrases are in the same order as they are in the text.**

1 There was a **huge fire** at our school yesterday. _____

2 Both the police and the fire service **dealt with** the problem. _____

3 The two cars **crashed into** each other. _____

4 How many **injured people** were there? _____

5 Firefighters face many **dangers** in their job. _____

# Grammar

## Passive: present, past and future

We use the passive voice when we are more interested in the action than the person doing it; when we are speaking in general; when we don't know who does the action; and when it is obvious who does the action. If we want to say who did the action, we use by.
*Hoax calls are made every day.*
*The new fire station was built next to the park.*
*The thief was arrested by police at the scene of the crime.*

The passive voice is formed by using the auxiliary verb be in the appropriate tense + the past participle of the main verb. We can use the following tenses in the passive voice: Present Simple, Present Continuous, Past Simple, Past Continuous, Present Perfect Simple, Past Perfect Simple, Future Simple, Future Perfect Simple and be going to.
*The situation is being investigated by the police right now.*
*All casualties have been given first-aid treatment.*
*This ambulance won't be used until further notice.*

**Note:** We don't use the passive voice in the Present Perfect Continuous, Past Perfect Continuous, Future Continuous or Future Perfect Continuous.

**A Underline examples of the passive voice in the text. Which tenses have been used?**

**B Change these sentences from active to passive voice.**

1 Storms often cause terrible damage.

2 They had involved the coastguard in the search.

3 Police were investigating the burglary at 9 am.

4 We moved the residents away from the burning building.

5 We'll bring food and water as soon as possible.

6 They're going to close down the old police station.

# Collocations

**Match.**

1 We must conduct     a   fire to things.

2 An ambulance was put on     b   court in a police van.

3 Police caught     c   stand-by at the festival.

4 Arsonists set     d   an investigation.

5 He was taken to     e   the streets.

6 Some policemen patrol     f   the thief red-handed.

# Speaking

**Work with a partner and answer these questions.**

1 What situations are shown in these photos?

2 Which emergency service(s) are involved in tackling each one?

3 What must the emergency services do in each case?

# Writing

**Write a short article about one of the emergencies in the Speaking task. Use the following paragraph plan.**

Para 1: Introduce the type of emergency.

Para 2: Say who it affects and which emergency service(s) deal(s) with it.

Para 3: Talk about preventative measures that could be taken.

**Discussion**

'The authorities must always be prepared for emergencies.' Discuss.

## Reading

Read the article about Hurricane Katrina. What would have helped the emergency services to be more successful in their efforts?

# Hurricane Katrina: the ruin of New Orleans

On 23rd August 2005, a tropical storm formed over the Bahamas. It increased in intensity until it became the cause of the most serious natural disaster the USA has ever experienced. (1) _____

With winds of over 275 km per hour, Katrina hit land just 70 km away from the city of New Orleans, Louisiana, on 29th August. Authorities in the city were at first relieved that the city wasn't hit directly by the storm. (2) _____ They weren't prepared for the fact that 80% of the city would be flooded by the following day.

In the days before the disaster, the authorities had monitored the storm as it moved towards Louisiana. (3) _____ This put into action Louisiana's rescue and recovery programme. People were asked to evacuate, and 1.2 million citizens left the city. But on the 28th, when a compulsory evacuation of the city was declared, tens of thousands of people were still there. Many couldn't be moved, while others refused to be evacuated.

After the hurricane hit the city and the surrounding area, relief workers, including voluntary workers and people from foreign aid agencies, flocked to the disaster zone. They battled on in terrible conditions to save people and get them to safety. (4) _____ Conditions became so unhygienic that a public health emergency was declared.

Unfortunately, the job of the emergency services was made even more difficult due to ineffective co-ordination. Many relief workers were left in doubt about what to do after receiving confusing information from different authorities. (5) _____

On 11th October, army engineers pumped out the last of the water from the city. By then, the death toll in Louisiana had risen to more than 1,400 and there were still thousands of people missing. (6) _____ While everyone accepts that the emergency services acted heroically, their efforts could have been even more successful if there had been proper co-ordination. Hurricane Katrina showed that much still needs to be learnt about managing large-scale emergencies.

## Comprehension

**Complete the article with these sentences.**

a   As a consequence, lives were lost that could have been saved.

b   In addition, approximately $100 billion worth of damage had been done.

c   It was named Hurricane Katrina.

d   Survivors had no food, water or other essentials.

e   Their relief came too early, however.

f   A state of emergency had been declared in New Orleans on the 27th.

**Guess what!**

One of the most unusual heroes from the time of Hurricane Katrina was a black Labrador retriever. The brave dog pulled a man from the flood waters to safety on higher ground. She was later named Katrina!

# Vocabulary

Complete the sentences with these words.

> death toll    declare    evacuation
> flock    intensity    monitor

1  All the emergency services helped in the _____ of the city.

2  Doctors must _____ the patient's condition for 24 hours.

3  Two days after the earthquake, the _____ had risen to 453.

4  Teams of firefighters will _____ to the disaster zone.

5  Fortunately, the _____ of the hurricane has decreased.

6  The mayor has decided to _____ a state of emergency.

# Grammar

## Passive: gerunds, infinitives and modals

The passive voice can be used with gerunds, infinitives and with modal verbs.
*He avoided being swept away in the storm.*
*Not all citizens were willing to be evacuated.*
*We could have been killed!*

**Note:** The verbs hear, see and make when it means force are followed by the bare infinitive in the active voice, but in the passive voice they are followed by the full infinitive.
*We make relief workers train constantly.*
*Relief workers are made to train constantly.*

**A  Look back at the article and underline every passive form which involves a gerund, an infinitive or a modal verb. Which of the three forms isn't in the article?**

**B  Circle the correct words.**

1  He was seen **to leave / leave** the accident without calling for help.

2  Nobody wanted **to be / being** left in the flooded town.

3  The death toll must **keep / be kept** to a minimum.

4  The officers hate not being **given / giving** specific orders by authorities.

5  The town should **have been / be** evacuated last week.

6  The survivors would rather **to have given / have been given** food and drink.

# Vocabulary

Complete the sentences with the correct form of **put** or **get**.

1  We must _____ all survivors to safety.

2  We must _____ the plan into action.

3  The paramedic _____ the casualty to stay still.

4  Don't _____ your head back as it'll make things worse.

5  Which position should we _____ him into?

6  We _____ a shock when we saw the extent of the damage.

# Listening

🎧 **Do the quiz, then listen and check your answers.**

1  You shouldn't hold ice to an injury for longer than
   a  two minutes.
   b  ten minutes.
   c  ten seconds.

2  How should a nosebleed be treated?
   a  by putting the victim's head back
   b  by putting the victim's head forward
   c  by putting cotton wool up the victim's nose

3  In Britain, what number can you **not** dial in an emergency?
   a  112
   b  911
   c  999

4  What must you **never** do for a burn?
   a  apply cream
   b  put the burn under cold water
   c  cover with a plastic bag

5  What is the first thing you should do if somebody is choking?
   a  push his/her tummy in
   b  check his/her mouth
   c  hit him/her on the back

6  What position should you put a casualty who has been saved from drowning into?
   a  with the head higher than the chest
   b  with the head on the same level as the chest
   c  with the head lower than the chest

## Prepositions

**Circle the correct words.**

1  Two million people **by / on / across** six countries have been affected.

2  The doctors are **on / in / for** doubt about how to treat the patient.

3  The survivors lived **in / of / for** terrible conditions.

4  Nobody was prepared **for / to / on** the earthquake.

5  They ran **in / on / out** fear of their lives.

**Skills 1: Listening and Speaking**

## Vocabulary

Write Pe (crime against a person), Pr (crime against property) or B (both).

1  arson ☐
2  armed robbery ☐
3  shoplifting ☐
4  blackmail ☐
5  burglary ☐
6  hit-and-run incident ☐
7  joyriding ☐
8  murder ☐
9  vandalism ☐
10  kidnapping ☐

## Listening skills

A  🎧 Listen to a conversation between two police officers who are patrolling the streets and make a note of all the police duties mentioned.

B  🎧 Listen to the conversation again. Write the crime being investigated by these officers.

1  Sunderland  _____
2  O'Malley  _____
3  Norman  _____
4  Anderson  _____
5  Hooper  _____

## Listening task

🎧 You will hear Detective Moran talking about crimes that have been committed. Which crime will each pair of officers investigate? For questions 1-5, write a letter (A-H) next to each pair. There are three letters which you do not need to use.

1  Bradley & Paterson ☐
2  Johnson & Riley ☐
3  Quinn & Spencer ☐
4  Brown & Cummings ☐
5  Jordan & Hughes ☐

A  burglary
B  armed robbery
C  joyriding
D  arson
E  hit-and-run incident
F  murder
G  shoplifting
H  kidnapping

110

### Giving your opinion

I believe/think …

In my opinion, …

The way I see it, …

To my mind, …

I'd suggest they receive/speak about …

My advice is for them to focus/concentrate on …

### Presenting arguments

… is/isn't a crime young people commit often.

… is a much more serious crime/issue than …

… isn't as serious as …, but it's common among …

… is a crime against property/a person, so …

… is/isn't very relevant to young people because …

# Listen Up!

🎧 Listen to two people discussing suitable punishments for crimes people have committed and answer the questions.

1 Who was given a warning?

2 Who thinks this punishment isn't fair? Why?

3 What punishment was given for vandalism?

4 How does the man feel about this punishment?

5 Which person supports tougher punishments for teenagers?

6 Which person do you agree with? Why?

# Speaking skills

A Tick the punishments that you think could be given to criminals sixteen years old and under.

1 prison sentence ☐

2 community service ☐

3 home detention ☐

4 fine ☐

5 driving license removed ☐

6 young offenders' institution ☐

7 warning ☐

B Complete these sentences using your own words.

1 In my opinion, young people who damage property …

2 I believe the first time a teenager commits a crime …

3 The way I see it, crimes against the person …

4 To my mind, community work …

5 I'd suggest joyriders are punished by …

6 My advice is for young people who repeatedly commit crimes to …

# Speaking tasks

A Look at the task in B below and make a note of what crimes each of the pictures show. Then rank each of the crimes from 1 (least) to 5 (most) to say:

a how serious it is.   b how relevant to young people it is.

_____    _____

_____    _____

_____    _____

_____    _____

_____    _____

B Some police officers from your area have been asked to come and speak to the students at your school about adolescent crime. Look at the pictures and work with a partner to decide which two the police officers should focus on.

Newspaper articles – who, what, where, when and how

 When we write newspaper articles about factual events we want to fully inform the readers about a situation. This means that we have to include details about who was involved, what happened, where, when and how an event happened.

**Read the following extracts from newspaper articles and answer the questions Who?, What?, Where?, When? and How? for each one.**

1 A twelve-year-old boy almost drowned this morning in the River Kelvin. The boy was cycling near the river when he hit a tree and fell into the water.

2 An office manager was given the sack yesterday because he hit a junior member of staff. The incident took place at *Key Mechanics*, which has been in the news in the past due to the inappropriate behaviour of its management.

## Writing task

**A Read the Writing task and make a list of possible incidents that might have happened.**

*Write a newspaper article about an incident that happened recently involving one or more of the emergency services.*

**B Read the model article and say who was involved, what happened, where, when and how the incident happened.**

*model composition*

# HUNDREDS OF FANS INJURED

**M**ore than 350 fans were rushed to hospital following violence at yesterday's football match between King's Park United and Coxton Town at the White Stadium. In spite of police efforts, a group of hooligans from King's Park managed to climb over fences between rival fans. They then angered Coxton supporters by throwing seats and other objects at them.

Police efforts to control the fans proved useless, despite the fact that they had been warned that an incident would occur. The fighting was finally stopped by the local fire brigade who used water jets to calm the crowd. Forty-two arrests were made.

An eyewitness said, 'I ran in fear of my life. Objects were flying at us from the King's Park supporters. I saw lots of people who were seriously injured and the paramedics couldn't get to them. Even though there were emergency exits, they were blocked in the chaos.'

A police spokesperson later commented that despite the introduction of more serious punishments for football hooligans, violence in stadiums is on the increase. She added that this is the second time this season that King's Park supporters have been involved in violence at a match. A full investigation will be conducted into yesterday's event.

# Analyse it!

**Underline the headline and examples of direct and indirect speech in the article. Then answer the questions.**

1 Which words are missing from the headline?

2 Why have they been missed out?

3 What effect does using direct speech in the article have?

4 What effect does using indirect speech in the article have?

5 Why has the passive voice been used?

# Writing plan

**Write the correct paragraph number from the model next to these descriptions.**

a Give an eye witness account of the incident. ☐

b Give further information about the background to the incident. ☐

c Report an expert's comment on the incident and say what action will be taken. ☐

d Say what, where, when and why the incident happened, who was involved and how it happened. ☐

# Grammar

### Even though, although, despite, in spite of

We use the linking words and phrases even though, although, despite and in spite of to introduce an idea that is the opposite of or contrasts with another idea. We follow even though and although with a subject and verb. We follow despite and in spite of with a noun, a pronoun or a gerund. Even though, although, despite and in spite of can come in the middle of a sentence between two clauses to show the contrast between them. There are no commas between the two clauses. They can also come at the beginning of the sentence but in this case we use commas to separate the two clauses.

*He dialled 999 even though/although nobody had been hurt.*
*Even though/Although she was injured, she didn't cry.*
*Despite/In spite of being a nurse, he didn't know what to do.*
*The firefighter rescued the man in spite of/despite the danger.*

> **Note:** We can use the fact (that) + subject and verb after despite and in spite of.
> *Despite/In spite of the fact that he was off duty, the officer did some investigating.*

**Choose the correct answers.**

1 _____ the roads were busy, the police arrived quickly.
  a Although    b In spite of    c Despite

2 _____ his injury, the thief kept running.
  a Although    b Despite    c In spite

3 The girl called for help even though she _____ it.
  a didn't need    b needed    c needing

4 A fire engine was sent in spite of _____ no fire.
  a being    b there was    c the fact there was

5 The man died in _____ the paramedic doing his best to save him.
  a spite of    b despite of    c despite

# Writing task

*Write a newspaper article about an incident that happened in your town.*

### Write right!

**Use these steps to help you write your article.**

**Step 1** Underline the key words in the task and decide what kind of incident you want to focus on.

**Step 2** Make notes about what happened, where, when and how it happened and who was involved.

**Step 3** Make a plan for your article and decide how you will organise the events. Use the plan opposite to help you.

**Step 4** Use your notes, your plan and the useful language above to write your article.

**Step 5** Read your article carefully when you have finished to check that it fully informs the reader about the incident. Make sure you have used the linking words *although*, *even though*, *despite* and *in spite of* properly.

## Discussion

'People who work for the emergency services are heroes.' Discuss this statement in relation to

a police officers.

b firefighters.

c paramedics.

# Review 5

## Vocabulary

### A Match.

1 manual worker ☐
2 breathing apparatus ☐
3 disaster zone ☐
4 fire hazard ☐
5 cutting equipment ☐

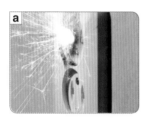

### B Complete the paragraph with these words.

casualties   damage   joyriding
property   tricks   vandalism

There are some crimes which young people are more likely to commit than others. These include (1) _____ , which involves damaging public or private (2) _____ ; (3) _____ , in which somebody steals a car in order to ride around in it for a while; and stupid (4) _____ such as making calls to the emergency services when nothing has happened. What these crimes have in common is that young people often see them as 'fun', but nothing could be less true. (5) _____ caused by vandals costs millions to repair every year, while riding around in stolen cars is even more serious as there are thousands of (6) _____ as a result of it. Hoax phone calls are no less damaging as they waste time and may mean that the emergency services are delayed in attending a real emergency.

### C Circle the odd one out.

| | | | |
|---|---|---|---|
| 1 | shoplifting | burglary | kidnapping |
| 2 | pocket money | scholarship | grant |
| 3 | economist | applicant | graduation |
| 4 | blaze | fire | vacancy |
| 5 | overalls | hard hat | drill |

### D Circle the correct words.

1 I don't want to do overtime / income.
2 Why don't you enrol / tackle on a computing course?
3 She wants to devote / economise herself to writing.
4 A fire engine was put out / on stand-by.
5 Christine shows / sets new staff the ropes.
6 Both of the bank robbers were given a ten-year prison sentence / evacuation.

## Grammar

### A Read the dialogue and complete the paragraph.

**Detective:** Tell me about the robbery yesterday, Miss Fit. Can you describe the robber?

**Witness:** I think so, Mr Lee. He was wearing large glasses, a green hat and a scarf.

**Detective:** Was he carrying anything?

**Witness:** Yes, he was carrying a green bag.

**Detective:** Hmm. There's a man of that description behind you.

**Witness:** Oh, that's him! That's the robber I saw!

The detective ordered the witness (1) _____ . He asked her (2) _____ the robber. The witness said that the robber (3) _____ large glasses, a green hat and a scarf. The detective asked (4) _____ anything. The witness said that (5) _____ a green bag. The detective said that (6) _____ a man of that description (7) _____ . The witness said that the man behind her was the robber she (8) _____ .

114

**B** Complete the second sentences using the words in bold. Use between two and five words.

1 The paramedic showed us how to put on a bandage.
**were**
We _____ how to put on a bandage by the paramedic.

2 We will interview ten people tomorrow.
**interviewed**
Ten people _____ tomorrow.

3 They only survived because they were wearing seat belts.
**killed**
They _____ if they hadn't been wearing seat belts.

4 They made Jonathon enrol on a training course.
**to**
Jonathon _____ enrol on a training course.

5 The company is making fifty people redundant today.
**by**
Fifty people _____ the company today.

6 We must evacuate the town by tomorrow.
**be**
The town _____ by tomorrow.

**C** Circle the correct words.

1 In despite / spite of the hurricane, they went sailing.

2 Imran applied for the job even although / though he wasn't qualified.

3 Although / In spite of she had done a lot of overtime, she wasn't tired.

4 Despite the fact that / being there was a recession, the company hired new staff.

5 Even though / Despite warnings from the police, they stayed at the scene of the accident.

# Strange but true!

The following stories are from real job interviews. Talk to a partner about why the job applicants wouldn't have been hired and say how they should have behaved.

Mum, do I usually arrive at work on time?

No, you're often late, dear.

**1** A twenty-year-old woman went for an interview as a teacher. She insisted that her mother was present during the interview and asked for her advice when answering the interviewer's questions.

**2** At an interview for the position of financial director at a large company, a man wore shorts, a colourful t-shirt and sandals.

**3** During an interview, an applicant was asked to fill in an application form. He took the form and lay down on the floor to complete it.

**4** An applicant who had an interview around noon told the interviewer that she hadn't had lunch yet. She then took out some fast food and ate it during the interview.

**5** A candidate was asked during an interview what his greatest achievement was. He replied that it was his collection of postage stamps.

**6** One job applicant was totally convinced she was the best person for the job. She even asked the interviewer to show her his CV to make sure he was qualified enough to interview her.

# 11 Music and Fashion

## Quiz

**Where is the world's largest Contemporary Performing Arts festival?**

a  New York, USA

b  Sydney, Australia

c  Glastonbury, UK

The Glastonbury Contemporary Performing Arts Festival, or Glastonbury, as it is usually called, is the largest of its kind in the world. It is held every year on a farm near Glastonbury, south-west England and attracts people of all ages. There are 80 stages and over 700 acts play over the five days of the festival. It is most famous for the pop music bands and solo artists who perform there, but you can hear other kinds of music and see theatre acts, comedy and dance as well. It attracts performers from all over the world and the site has a capacity for over 177,000 spectators. Many famous people go to the festival and it is a fashionable event to go to and be seen at.

Discussion

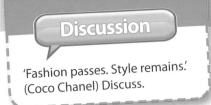

'Fashion passes. Style remains.'
(Coco Chanel) Discuss.

## Reading

**Read the film review. Were all of the costumes made specially for the film? How do we know?**

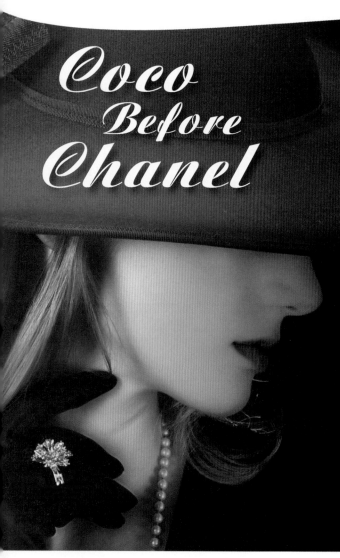

*Coco Before Chanel*

Numerous films about the fashion industry have been made in the past. (1) _____ These films attempt to reveal the superficial nature of the fashion business and those who work in it. *Coco Before Chanel*, written and directed by Anne Fontaine, however, isn't as stereotypical as these films.

Based on the early life of fashion designer Coco Chanel, this drama tells the story of Chanel's incredible journey to fame and fortune. The plot begins just after Coco, whose real name was Gabrielle, leaves the orphanage where her father left her. In order to survive, she works as a seamstress making costumes. Coco's life changes dramatically when she meets Baron Balsan and is introduced to his wealthy friends. (2) _____

Actress Audrey Tautou is very good in the role of talented but cynical Chanel. She manages to give a realistic performance of the most stylish female designer in the fashion world. She shows Chanel as being ahead of her time and as a woman who doesn't let herself be limited by current fashions. (3) _____ For Chanel, fashion wasn't about following trends, but about showing who you really are.

One of the things followers of fashion may be let down by in the film is, surprisingly, the costumes. (4) _____ Fontaine has deliberately kept glamour out of the picture to reflect Chanel's early designs. In fact some of the costumes worn are actually the original clothes designed by Chanel.

(5) _____ However, it is a well-made film about the life of a remarkable woman, who achieved success against all odds.

## Comprehension

**Complete the review with these sentences.**

a   It's only a matter of time before she starts designing for them.

b   Overall, *Coco Before Chanel* is unlikely to be a blockbuster.

c   *Zoolander*, *The Devil Wears Prada* and *Pret a Porter* are just some of the recent box-office successes.

d   However, given that the film is set in the years before Chanel made a name for herself, the style is appropriate.

e   This attitude comes out in her designs which aren't as soft and pretty as mainstream fashions of the day.

## Vocabulary

**Circle the correct words.**

1   Why are you so cynical / stereotypical about this designer?

2   He doesn't design superficial / mainstream clothes.

3   Was this film an orphanage / a blockbuster?

4   That model has got a bad glamour / attitude.

5   Is this a realistic / numerous drawing of Chanel?

# Grammar

## Adjectives

When we use two or more adjectives before a noun, the adjectives usually follow this order: opinion, size, age, shape, colour, origin, material.
*She was wearing a beautiful, green, cotton scarf.*
*I love those huge, new, Spanish high heels.*

We can use adjectives after verbs like appear, be, become, feel, get, look, make, seem, smell, sound, taste and turn. Sometimes we put an adverb between the verb and the adjective.
*Jack isn't trendy.*
*Their new CD sounds fantastic.*
*The designer seems very unhappy with the clothes.*

## Comparison of adjectives

We can use the comparative to compare two or more people or things or two or more groups of people or things.
*Carla's coat is warmer than Jackie's.*
*French perfumes tend to be more expensive than perfumes from other countries.*

We can use the superlative to compare someone or something to other people or things.
*Who's the most talented member of the band?*
*She's the best guitarist we could find.*

We can use as + adjective + as to compare two people or things that are similar. We can use not as + adjective + as to compare two people or things that are different.
*This shampoo is as good as the expensive one.*
*The fashion show isn't as exciting as the last one I went to.*

We can use the + comparative ..., the + comparative to show that something is influenced by how much something else increases or decreases.
*The less he sleeps, the worse he looks.*
*The more he sings, the better he becomes.*

### A  Circle the correct answers.

1  These boots aren't as warm / warmer as my old ones.

2  Whose is this silk, long, red / long, red, silk coat?

3  This year's catalogue looks great / the most great!

4  The more I look at the bag, the most / more I like it.

5  The red blouse is prettier / the prettiest in your wardrobe.

6  The band's new video is worse from / than their last one.

### B  Complete the sentences with -, the, than, as or not as.

1  The radio station is _____ further than I expected.

2  That was _____ best video clip I've seen.

3  Modelling's tough and _____ glamorous as you think.

4  The colder it gets, _____ more clothes I need to wear.

5  The silk trousers are nicer _____ the jeans.

6  This model is as beautiful _____ Kate Moss.

# Word formation

### A  Complete the table.

| Verb | Noun | Adjective |
|---|---|---|
| (1) _____ | designer | designed |
| (2) _____ | complication | complicated |
| limit | (3) _____ | limited |
| perfect | perfection | (4) _____ |
| compose | (5) _____ | composed |
| improvise | improvisation | (6) _____ |

### B  Complete the sentences with some of the words from A.

1  The designer always tries to achieve _____ .

2  The design might look simple, but it's actually _____ .

3  She plays well, but her acting ability is _____ .

4  Is the_____ of this handbag well-known?

5  He must _____ at least three new songs for his album.

6  We'll have to _____ because we don't have time to rehearse.

# Speaking

### A  Rank the following things from 1 to 4 with 1 being the most important criterion for buying clothes and 4 being the least. Then explain your choices to your partner.

comfort ____        price      ____
make      ____        trendiness ____

### B  Look at the following clothes and accessories. Say which you would wear and which you would recommend for your partner.

# Writing

Write a short description of the type of clothes your partner wears and his/her attitude to fashion.

**Discussion**

'Live music is a dying art.' Discuss.

## Reading

Read the article about music in Greece. How would you describe the writer's attitude towards Greek music?

# Greek Beat

There's something uplifting about listening to live music. For thousands of years people have been composing, playing and listening to music. In ancient Greek theatre, for example, live music was a very important element. This is a tradition that still remains in modern Greece.

Despite what visitors to Greece may think, Greek music doesn't start and stop with the bouzouki. In fact, it is extremely varied. There are several genres including folk, nisiotika (songs from the islands), new wave, hip hop, rock and pop. Many regions also proudly produce their own distinctive sound. For instance, traditional music from the Ipirus region is very different to music from the northern areas of Macedonia and Thessaly.

Another indication of the variety in Greek music is the numerous instruments used in creating it. String instruments include the oud, lyre, baglama (a miniature bouzouki), guitar and violin. Wind instruments are represented by the clarinet, accordion, flute and bagpipes amongst others, while percussion instruments include the doumbek (a drum held under the arm), the daouli (a kind of bass drum) and the defi, which is like a tambourine. It's not unusual for Greeks to play at least one of these instruments.

One of the real beauties of live Greek music, however, is that it is often spontaneous and improvised. Many Greeks never pass up the chance to get out their instruments and break into song inside their local cafés or during celebrations and social events like weddings and birthdays. There are hundreds of popular songs they can sing which have been passed down from generation to generation. Songs about hard times, songs of celebration and songs of glory have all been kept alive. In a way, these songs help to connect people with their past as well as create a common culture today.

In recent years the popularity of electronic music has greatly risen in Greece, but that hasn't stopped youngsters from taking up an instrument. The creation of public music schools by the Greek government has meant that those who are dedicated to music have the chance to develop their talents every day at school. Hopefully, this will allow the tradition of playing live music to continue for years to come.

## Comprehension

**Write A if the sentence is correct and B if it is not correct.**

1   Live music is not an element of modern Greek theatre. ☐

2   The bouzouki is used in all kinds of Greek music. ☐

3   A baglama is a smaller version of a bouzouki. ☐

4   Performances of Greek music aren't always rehearsed. ☐

5   Greek children are only interested in electronic music. ☐

6   Children with musical talent can now attend special schools. ☐

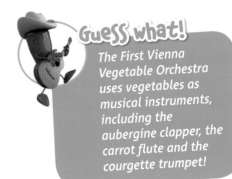

**Guess what!**

The First Vienna Vegetable Orchestra uses vegetables as musical instruments, including the aubergine clapper, the carrot flute and the courgette trumpet!

# Vocabulary

Find words in the article that have these meanings. The words are in the same order as they appear in the text.

1  inspiring, moving  _____

2  part, aspect  _____

3  characteristic  _____

4  sign  _____

5  not planned  _____

6  success, triumph  _____

# Grammar

## Adverbs (manner, place, time, degree)

Adverbs of manner (slowly, fast, beautifully, nicely, easily, quickly, etc) tell us how something happens.
*They performed the song too fast.*

Adverbs of place (here, there, inside, outside, beside, opposite, in the cinema, etc) tell us where something happens.
*We've decided to have the concert outside.*

Adverbs of time (yesterday, today, tomorrow, later, last year, etc) tell us when something happens.
*Are you meeting the director tomorrow?*

Adverbs of degree (enough, quite, rather, too, so, absolutely, etc) tell us how much or how many there is of something or the extent of something.
*The record company is absolutely delighted with your latest work.*

Note: When there's more than one adverb in a sentence, they normally appear in this order: manner, place, time.
*The fans waited excitedly outside the concert hall.*

When the sentence has a verb of movement (eg come, go, walk), they usually appear in this order: place, manner, time. The adverb of manner can also go before the main verb.
*He left the stage slowly. = He slowly left the stage.*

## Comparison of adverbs

Adverbs which are the same as adjectives (early, fast, hard, high, late) have the same comparative and superlative form as the adjectives.
*Let's try our hardest to make the best video clip ever!*

When adverbs end in –ly, we use more in the comparative form and the most in the superlative form.
*Does Anna sing more beautifully than Katie?*

**A  Look at the words and phrases highlighted in the article and label each one an adverb of manner, place, time or degree.**

---

**B  Circle the correct words.**

1  The drummer shouted at us angrily / extremely.

2  I sing well but I dance badly / worse.

3  Please wait for me absolutely / outside.

4  I've seen that guitarist before / later.

5  He stood nervously on stage earlier / earlier on stage nervously.

# Vocabulary

Circle the odd one out.

| 1 | clarinet | flute | tambourine |
|---|----------|-------|------------|
| 2 | lyrics | words | songwriter |
| 3 | varied | different | social |
| 4 | improvise | compose | write |
| 5 | sound check | busking | dress rehearsal |

# Listening

🎧 **Listen and number the pictures in the correct order.**

## Phrasal verbs

**Complete the sentences with around, by, down, for, on or up.**

1  We passed _____ the singer's house.

2  This drum was passed _____ to me by my father.

3  Can you pass _____ a message to the producer?

4  I didn't pass _____ the chance to go backstage!

5  You pass _____ a teenager in those clothes.

6  Helga's passing _____ copies of the lyrics.

## Vocabulary

**Circle the correct answers.**

1  I like to be different. I always wear _____ clothes.
   a  mainstream    b  wacky      c  trendy

2  _____ to the magazine get into *Fashion World* free.
   a  Catwalks    b  Trendsetters  c  Subscribers

3  Look! He's torn the jacket to his _____ .
   a  tuxedo      b  bow-tie    c  denims

4  Patent _____ shoes are very shiny.
   a  suede      b  velvet      c  leather

5  I like flowers, but this _____ print dress is awful!
   a  embroidered    b  floral      c  plaid

6  Wear straight-legged jeans because those _____ ones don't look nice.
   a  square      b  luminous    c  baggy

7  Should I wear the _____ top?
   a  pump      b  high-heeled    c  polo-neck

8  Oh no! I've spilt the _____ again.
   a  dyes      b  silks      b  ovals

## Listening skills

A  🎧 **Listen to a conversation between Zoe and Jamil and write down phrases or sentences they use which mean the same as the following.**

1  isn't just concerned with  _____

2  I don't believe it!  _____

3  You may learn some useful things.  _____

4  I'll take you.  _____

B  🎧 **Listen to the conversation again and complete the sentences.**

1  *It Teens* magazine isn't just concerned with _____ . It also includes music.

2  Jamil doesn't believe Zoe got a _____ of the *Humanoid* CD.

3  Zoe says Jamil may learn some useful _____ at the fashion show.

4  Zoe offers to take Jamil to the show on her _____ .

## Listening task

🎧 **Listen and complete the notes.**

1  *It Teens* magazine has _____ the fashion show.

2  Models of all _____ will show off Paz's designs.

3  The trousers Lee is wearing have got _____ on the thighs.

4  There are three colours of tuxedo available: light blue, _____ and _____ .

5  The front of Alina's top is covered in _____ .

6  The white dress took _____ to complete.

### Describing people

**Feelings**

He/She looks/seems/appears to be afraid/anxious/cheerful/confident/dreamy/happy/guilty/indifferent/sad/thoughtful

**Size**

He/She is very tall/small in height/of small/medium/large build/chubby/slender.

It is big/huge/tiny/miniature.

**Clothes and appearance**

He/She is wearing …

He/She has got … on.

He/She/It looks elegant/wacky/fashionable/trendy/ridiculous/old-fashioned/uncomfortable/impractical

## Listen Up!

🎧 Listen to Simon describing a picture and tick the pictured described. What details helped you to choose?

## Speaking skills

A Work with a partner and take it in turns to describe one of the pictures in each pair and guess which picture your partner is describing.

1a

1b

2a

2b

B Answer the questions.

1 What are the differences between the picture your partner described and the other one in the pair?

2 Which words and phrases used by your partner helped you to choose the correct picture?

## Speaking tasks

A Look at the pictures in B and write down as many adjectives as you can connected to them.

B Work with a partner and take it in turns to describe what the people are doing in these pictures and say how you think they are feeling. Student A should talk about picture 1 and Student B should talk about picture 2.

1

2

C Do you think young people worry too much about their appearance?

## Expressing positive and negative ideas

 In essays, you are often asked to talk about the advantages, disadvantages or both of an activity or an idea. The language that we use to discuss benefits is different to the language that we use to describe drawbacks. When presenting positive ideas, we use the affirmative form of verbs; verbs like improve, allow and create; nouns like advantage and benefit; and positive adjectives and adverbs like marvellous, happily and gladly. When presenting negative ideas, we use the negative form of verbs; verbs like harm, damage and prevent; nouns like disadvantage and drawback; and negative adjectives and adverbs like annoying, embarrassing, frustrating, terribly and unfortunately.

**Read these sentences about listening to the radio and decide whether they present ideas in a positive or negative way.**

1 You can easily find different radio stations to listen to.

2 It can be very annoying when the DJ speaks over a track.

3 Listening to the radio allows you to feel that you have company.

4 Another drawback is that the music is often interrupted with adverts.

5 It is possible to listen to the radio almost anywhere.

6 Apart from the initial cost of the radio, listening to music on the radio is completely free.

# Writing task

**A Read the Writing task and answer the questions.**

*Write an essay which discusses the benefits of young people learning to play a musical instrument.*

1 What are the key words in the task?

2 Will the essay discuss disadvantages? Why?/Why not?

3 Can you think of any advantages of playing instruments?

4 Are these advantages just for musicians or for other people as well?

**B Read the model essay and underline words and phrases that express ideas in a positive way. Why do you think the writer has presented his arguments in the order they are in the middle three paragraphs?**

## The benefits of playing an instrument

 model composition

Taking up a musical instrument has many advantages for young people. Let us look at some of them.

Firstly, studies show that learning to play a musical instrument can improve general intelligence. At school, musical students usually have higher grades in maths and science. This is because it is essential to use a way of thinking also needed in these subjects when they are playing an instrument.

Furthermore, playing an instrument has an effect on young people's character. First of all, it makes them more patient and disciplined. Musicians get into the habit of practising for a certain amount of time and therefore learn to focus. In addition, both listening to and playing music helps people to cope with stress as it makes them feel calmer.

Finally, young musicians have an interesting and creative way of expressing themselves. They never need to feel bored as they can pick up their guitar or sit at the piano and create music.

In conclusion, there are many benefits of learning to play an instrument for young people. It not only helps them be creative, but also has positive effects in other areas such as with their school work and well-being.

# Analyse it!

**Write T (true) or F (false).**

1 The writer says what the essay will be about in the introduction. ☐

2 The writer has used some negative language. ☐

3 The writer has made a mistake by not discussing the disadvantages. ☐

4 The writer has provided a long list of instruments young people can play. ☐

5 The essay is written in a formal style. ☐

# Writing plan

**Write the correct paragraph number from the model next to these descriptions.**

a Conclude by briefly restating the arguments made. ☐

b Discuss the advantages concerning creativity. ☐

c Discuss the advantages concerning schoolwork. ☐

d Inform the reader what you're going to talk about. ☐

e Discuss the advantages concerning character. ☐

# Grammar

### Adjectives ending in -ing/-ed

Some adjectives can be formed using the present participle ending –ing and the past participle ending –ed. The –ing form is active and describes the effect someone or something has on others. The –ed form is passive and describes how someone or something is affected by something or how they feel about it.

*The singer is amusing. = The singer's funny.*
*The singer is amused. = The singer thinks something is funny.*
*He was embarrassed. = He felt bad about something.*
*He was embarrassing. = Other people thought he did something bad.*

### Adjectives and infinitives

Adjectives can often be followed by the full infinitive. Sometimes there is an object or a noun after the adjective.

*Going to a live concert is a marvellous way to spend the evening.*
*It's essential to give the seamstress your measurements by Tuesday.*

**Rewrite the sentences using the words in bold. Use between two and five words.**

1 I couldn't pull up the zip no matter how hard I tried.
It was _____ up the zip. **impossible**

2 We thought the DVD was amusing.
We _____ by the DVD. **were**

3 Seeing such a big audience is encouraging for us.
We're _____ such a big audience. **to**

4 I find his songs really annoying.
I _____ with his songs. **get**

5 You shouldn't have promised that she could sing.
It was _____ that she could sing. **wrong**

# Writing task

*Write an essay discussing the disadvantages of listening only to pop music.*

## Write right!

**Use these steps to help you write your essay.**

**Step 1** Underline the key words in the task and make a list of possible disadvantages to write about.

**Step 2** Decide on two or three disadvantages to focus on and make notes about why they are negative. Do any research necessary to find out more about the topic.

**Step 3** Make a plan for your essay and decide how you will organise the ideas. Use the plan opposite to help you.

**Step 4** Use your notes, your plan and the useful language above to write your essay.

**Step 5** Read your essay carefully when you have finished to check that it deals only with disadvantages and that you have used suitable language to express them.

## Discussion

'Your taste in music and fashion reveals a lot about your personality.' Discuss.

# 12 Mysteries

This aerial view of Stonehenge in Wiltshire, England, shows the circular arrangement of the giant stones that form the ancient site. Stonehenge dates from about 4,500 years ago and it is one of the most famous sites in the world. While its exact function still remains a mystery, many theories have been put forward by archaeologists. Amongst these are the ideas that the site was a place of healing or a place from which the night sky could be admired. Another mystery surrounding the site is how the massive stones were transported there, considering their size and the lack of a practical means of transport at the time.

How many hours of work was needed to construct Stonehenge?

a  about 3,000
b  about 30,000
c  about 30 million

## Lesson 1

**Discussion**

'A good detective must be a good judge of character.' Discuss.

## Reading

**Read the mystery on the website. Who do you think stole the Easer Tiara?**

a  Lord and Lady Easer       b  The cook and the butler       c  The maid and the cook

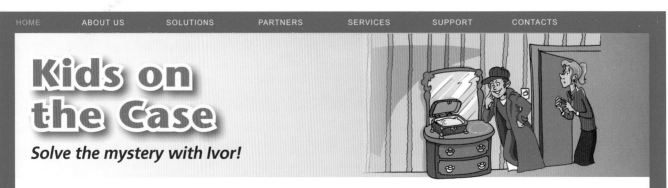

HOME        ABOUT US        SOLUTIONS        PARTNERS        SERVICES        SUPPORT        CONTACTS

# Kids on the Case

*Solve the mystery with Ivor!*

Cadborton's famous sleuth, Ivor Clue, arrived at the Easer Mansion. The Easer Tiara, which had been in the family for centuries, had been stolen.

Lady Easer met Ivor in the hall where she was walking up and down nervously. Ivor introduced himself and asked what had happened.

'It's unbelievable!' said Lady Easer. 'I saw the tiara in its box at 3 pm, but when I looked again at four it was gone! I can't understand it because I didn't leave the room at all. Three people came in but I don't see how they could have taken it. It's far too big to conceal in your clothes. Today is my birthday and the maid arrived with some flowers from a friend of mine just after three. I told her that I wanted to have a rest and to tell the staff not to bother me again, but she can't have told the cook because she came at about three thirty. She insisted on showing me the birthday cake she'd made. I took a quick look and dismissed her. The butler phoned to ask if I needed anything just before the cook left. I was furious and I told him I just wanted to be left by myself for a while. Anyway, around ten to four my husband popped in, and shortly afterwards I noticed the tiara was gone.'

'Hmm. Can I see your room, please?' asked Ivor.

As Lady Easer led Ivor up the stairs, he took the chance to look around at the crumbling mansion, which was in need of serious repairs. It crossed his mind that the tiara could have been hidden by Lord and Lady Easer themselves to get their hands on some much-needed insurance money.

When they arrived in the dining room, Lady Easer pointed out the empty box on the dresser. Ivor went over to inspect it. He saw that in the space next to the box the dust had been disturbed by something circular and there was a trace of white powder. He sniffed the powder and then sampled it, deciding that it was icing sugar. He looked over at the phone on the desk at the other side of the room and a thought occurred to him. 'Can you see the dresser when you're on the phone?' he asked.

'Well, no,' said Lady Easer. 'The desk faces the opposite wall.'

'Please come with me to the kitchen, Lady Easer,' Ivor said. 'I believe I have worked out what happened. I am confident that the tiara is inside the cake. And I think we'll find there are two criminals, not just one.'

## Comprehension

**The words in bold are wrong. Write the correct words.**

1  Lady Easer was waiting for Ivor in the **dining room**.          _____

2  The flowers were sent by Lady's Easer's **maid**.               _____

3  Lady Easer was **pleased** when the butler rang.               _____

4  Lady Easer's husband arrived at **three thirty**.              _____

5  Ivor thinks that Lord and Lady Easer may have **given away** the tiara.   _____

6  Ivor is **not certain** that he knows where the tiara is.       _____

# Vocabulary

**Find the words on the website and circle the correct meaning, a or b.**

1 rest
    a period of relaxation      b remains of something

2 dismissed
    a sacked      b sent away

3 disturbed
    a interrupted      b moved

4 dresser
    a someone who dresses others   b a piece of furniture

5 sampled
    a analysed      b tasted

6 confident
    a sure of one's ability      b sure one is right

# Grammar

## Pronouns (reflexive, indefinite and possessive)

Reflexive pronouns (myself, yourself, himself, herself, itself, oneself, ourselves, yourselves and themselves) are used as the object of verbs when the subject and the object of an action are the same. They can be used after a verb + preposition. They can also be used to emphasise nouns.
*I blame myself for not warning them about the danger.*
*How did the investigators lock themselves out of the room?*
*The young sleuth solved the mystery herself!*

Indefinite pronouns (eg anybody, anyone, anything, everybody, everyone, everything, nobody, no one, nothing, somebody, someone, something) are used to replace nouns without making it clear which nouns they replace.
*Someone has stolen my purse!*
*There's nothing you can do about crime.*
*Does anybody want to solve this mystery?*

Possessive pronouns (mine, yours, his, hers, ours, theirs) show who something belongs to and avoid repetition of the noun.
*This magnifying glass is mine, not hers.*

**Note:** We don't usually use its as a possessive pronoun.

**A Underline examples of reflexive, indefinite and possessive pronouns on the website. Say what kind of pronoun each one is and which noun it replaces or refers to.**

# B Complete the paragraph with these words.

| anything | hers | herself |
| nothing | somebody | themselves |

Anna sighed as she stood alone in the room with the strange statues. Once again an acquaintance of (1) _____ had asked for her help with a mystery. She promised (2) _____ this would be her last case. She had just moved to a new town and she wanted to lead a normal life. But, whenever (3) _____ out of the ordinary happened, she always seemed to be first on the scene. (4) _____ had even said that she could smell trouble. So far the locals weren't aware that Anna was a gifted sleuth. They (5) _____ were under the impression that she was an ordinary woman and they knew (6) _____ about Anna's mystery-solving talents. Anna was hoping to keep it that way.

# Collocations

**Choose the correct answers.**

1 I promise we'll get to the _____ of the actor's strange disappearance.
    a bottom      b base      c end

2 Who made Stonehenge remains a _____ to this day.
    a puzzle      b mystery      c thriller

3 The man's behaviour is out of the _____ .
    a ordinary      b usual      c normal

4 Has it _____ your mind that I might be innocent?
    a passed      b arrived      c crossed

5 What _____ have you drawn from analysing these samples?
    a assumptions      b answers      c conclusions

6 The thief wanted to get his _____ on the jewels.
    a hands      b faces      c fingers

# Speaking

**Work with a partner and answer the questions.**

1 Can you name three mysteries, myths or legends?

2 Which is your favourite one and why?

# Writing

**Write a short story about a mystery, a myth or a legend for the *Kids on the Case* website.**

**Discussion**

'There are some mysteries that can never be solved.' Discuss.

## Reading

**Read the article about the Dabous petroglyph. Which physical characteristics of giraffes are mentioned?**

# Secrets of the sand: The Dabous Giraffes

The vast Tenere Desert is a mysterious land. In 1987, one of its best kept secrets was revealed: the giraffe petroglyph in Dabous, Niger. The strange petroglyph, or stone carving, depicts two life-sized giraffes with lines coming down from their mouths and people attached to the ends. This remarkable work of pre-historic art is at the top of a sandstone rock high above the ground.

Who created the petroglyph is a mystery that still hasn't been solved. It is possible that the artists were Kiffians, who were pre-historic inhabitants of the Sahara. The Kiffians were hunters who died out 8,000 years ago due to drought. It is also possible that the artists were Tenerians, occupants of the area 7,000 years ago when there was rainfall in the Sahara.

The creators, whoever they were, used techniques such as engraving and scraping the sandstone as well as making parts of it smooth. Given that it was created before the Bronze Age, this would probably have been done with flint stone, as metal wasn't used until much later. During its creation care must have been taken in selecting its position. The petroglyph is only visible by climbing up on top of the rock and looking down on it.

What really puzzles scientists, though, is what the giraffe scene might have meant to its creators. Some suggest that giraffes were chosen because of their beauty. They are unique among animals and are tall but graceful. Others believe that there must have been a less trivial reason for the choice. Their theory is that giraffes were of great symbolic value to the society. Giraffes have got large eyes and due to their height can see great distances. Consequently, they see danger coming from far away. Were giraffes carved to pay respect to these capabailities? Was this in the hope that people could benefit from their ability to see far away to predict events to come? If so, this could also explain the lines linking people to the giraffes.

The Dabous petroglyph is one of many in this area. Scientists have been working hard for years to try and put together the pieces of this puzzle in order to uncover the history of the region, and nobody knows what they will discover in the future. For the time being, all they can do is wonder what other secrets the desert is concealing.

## Comprehension

**Answer the questions.**

1. When was the Dabous petroglyph discovered?
2. Who might have carved the petroglyph?
3. What happened to the Kiffians?
4. How do we know the carving wasn't done using metal tools?
5. Why might the giraffe have been highly respected in the past?
6. Why are scientists interested in art like the Dabous petroglyph?

**Guess what!**

The Nazca lines of Peru form outlines of animals that can only be seen from high above, yet they were made approximately 2,000 years ago, well before man could fly!

# Vocabulary

**Find words in the article which mean the same as the words in bold. The words are in the same order as they appear in the text.**

1  The cave painting **shows** two cows. _____
2  In this picture the dogs are **joined** to each other. _____
3  They **disappeared** a hundred years ago. _____
4  Who are the **inhabitants** of the area? _____
5  Who were the **makers** of this art? _____

# Grammar

## Review of Tenses

**A  Identify each of the tenses used in the sentences below.**

1  We've been coming here for ten years.
2  Will they discover the truth soon?
3  Are they going to solve the mystery?
4  Nobody has ever seen the Yeti.
5  The treasure was buried in 1765.
6  This time tomorrow we'll be sleeping.
7  Scientists disagree about the cause of the disease.
8  The boy had vanished before she got there.
9  Look! A satellite is flying across the sky!
10  Jason will have returned by Tuesday.
11  We were watching the documentary at 5.30.
12  He'll have been missing for six hours soon.
13  He'd been living in Japan for two years.

**B  Look at the verbs highlighted in the article. Which tenses are they in? Are they active or passive? Why have these tenses been used?**

**C  Circle the correct words.**

1  How long will it take / be taking them to arrive?
2  Giraffes have lived / live here for centuries.
3  What did the detective see / was the detective seeing?
4  They haven't / hadn't been able to solve the mystery yet.
5  We hadn't gone / didn't go far when the accident happened.
6  The evidence points / is pointing to one thing.
7  Quick, run! The thief will / is going to escape!
8  I saw a lots of antiques while I was visiting / visited the castle.

# Vocabulary

**Complete the word groups.**

| convincing | graceful |      |
| --- | --- | --- |
| smooth | trivial | vast |

1  flat          even          _____
2  unimportant   superficial   _____
3  huge          enormous      _____
4  elegant       stylish       _____
5  believable    persuasive    _____

# Listening

🎧 **Circle the correct words.**

1  Dutch explorers arrived on Easter Island 500 years ago / in 1722 / in 1995.
2  In the past, the island had about 16 million inhabitants / buildings / trees.
3  The speaker says the Polynesians used trees for fuel / statues / weapons for war.
4  There are 10 / 400 / 887 statues on Easter Island.
5  The moai statues look like people / elephants / aliens.
6  Eric von Daniken claims the statues were made in a volcano / space / a forest.

## Prepositions

**The words in bold are wrong. Write the correct words.**

1  I'm glad we're all **on** agreement about the origin of the ring. _____
2  Don't keep secrets **for** me. Tell me! _____
3  Why must we pay respect **of** these animals? _____
4  **From** theory, the mystery can be solved. _____
5  It may look easy to solve, but **at** practice it is impossible. _____

## Vocabulary

Complete the collocations with these words.

| ball | bat | circle | city | costume | illusion | Monster | object | Snowman | Triangle |

1  optical _____
2  crop _____
3  Loch Ness _____
4  Lost _____ of Atlantis
5  unidentified flying _____

6  vampire _____
7  Bermuda _____
8  Halloween _____
9  Abominable _____
10  crystal _____

## Listening skills

A  🎧 Listen to two people talking about strange phenomena and tick all the things from the vocabulary task above which are mentioned.

B  🎧 Listen again and write Y (yes), N (no) or DK (don't know).

1  The Abominable Snowman is also known as The Yeti. ☐
2  Halloween is on the 30th September. ☐
3  The Bermuda Triangle is an optical illusion. ☐
4  Crop circles are definitely made by people. ☐

## Listening task

🎧 Listen and tick (✓) the correct pictures.

1  Where is the game now?

 a   b   c

2  What does the box contain?

 a   b   c

3  When was the UFO first seen?

 a   b   c

4  How will they travel to the caves?

 a   b  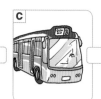 c

5  Which film isn't showing?

 a   b   c

6  When will the couple go to Macchu Picchu?

 a   b   c

## express yourself!

### Expressing preferences

… is not particularly interesting/mysterious.

… is (un)suitable/(un)acceptable for young people …

… would(n't) go down well with …, because …

… is by far the best choice because …

… is the kind of thing young people go for/enjoy/like.

Young people would much rather + bare infinitive /prefer + full infinitive/noun …

## Listen Up!

🎧 **Listen to a conversation in a shop and answer the questions.**

1   Why does the girl reject the first three ideas?

2   What does she decide to buy in the end? Why?

## Speaking skills

**A   Look at the pictures in B. What mysteries are shown? Choose one and make a note of words and phrases you associate with it.**

**B   Work with a partner and take turns at describing one of the mysteries suggested in the pictures below. Tell your partner as much as you can about the mystery and say how interesting it is for young people and why.**

## Speaking tasks

**A   Read the Speaking task in B and look at the pictures below. Talk to your partner about what suggestion each picture shows and then rank them from 1-5, with 1 being the most interesting and 5 being the least interesting.**

1   _____

2   _____

3   _____

4   _____

5   _____

**B   A friend of yours works for the school magazine and wants to publish an issue about mysteries. Look at the pictures and work with a partner to discuss possible topics the magazine could cover and decide which two are most suitable.**

133

## Qualifiers

 Qualifiers are words or phrases that appear before an adjective or an adverb that increase or decrease the intensity of the adjective or adverb. Some qualifiers are extreme (eg absolutely, completely, entirely, totally, utterly) and can only be used with extreme adjectives and adverbs (eg amazing, awful ,enormous, essential, excellent, freezing, furious, impossible, ridiculous). Some other qualifiers (eg a bit, extremely, highly, rather, slightly, so, much, very) can only be used with adjectives or adverbs that are gradable (eg angry, big, busy, disgusting, frightening, important, (un)likely, mysterious, recommended).

The qualifiers fairly, pretty, really and quite can be used with both extreme and gradable adjectives and adverbs.

**Circle the correct words.**

1 This film about monsters is totally / very long.

2 This book is completely / rather frightening.

3 I was absolutely / slightly freezing in the haunted house in the forest.

4 It's completely / extremely impossible to solve the mystery.

5 You look very / utterly ridiculous in that costume!

6 Sherlock is a bit / entirely busy at the moment.

# Writing task

**A Read the writing task and underline the kind of text you will read in the model. What information must the writer provide?**

*This is part of an email you received from an English-speaking friend.*

> In your postcard you say that you saw something really bizarre when you were on holiday. What was it? Is there an explanation for it?

*Write an email answering your friend's questions.*

**B Read the model email and underline any qualifiers used. Say whether each qualifier is used with an extreme or gradable adjective or adverb.**

*model composition*

Hi Kate,

I'm extremely pleased you got the postcard from my holiday in Ireland. Isn't the picture absolutely stunning? It's of the River Blackwater and Lismore Castle in County Waterford.

Anyway, let me tell you about an adventure I had there. We were staying at a hotel in Waterford while on a hiking tour of the Comeragh Mountains. The owner was such a sweet lady and she gave us lots of advice about what to see and do. She told us we must visit Mystery Road. My sister and I were pretty interested and talked Dad into hiring a car for the day to go there.

On the way, the scenery was really amazing. We drove for about an hour through green valleys and down winding roads. We were going down a slight hill when we suddenly arrived at the famous tree. The hotel owner had told us that we should stop there. Dad stopped the car but he didn't put the break on. We then had such a bizarre experience. We expected the car to go downhill, but it started rolling uphill!

Mystery Road is actually an optical illusion. The way the road has been cut into the surrounding land makes it look as if it's going up when it's actually going down. It's so weird!

That's all for now. Write soon.

Love,

Isabella

# Analyse it!

**Tick (✓) what the writer has done in the email.**

1 written a postcard ☐
2 attached a holiday photo ☐
3 written about a bizarre experience ☐
4 provided an explanation for the experience ☐
5 written in an informal style ☐
6 used qualifiers to make it more interesting ☐

# Writing plan

**Match.**

1 Greeting
2 Paragraph 1
3 Paragraph 2
4 Paragraph 3
5 Paragraph 4
6 Paragraph 5
7 Signing off

a Give background details to the story.
b Give an explanation for the strange event.
c Love, Isabella
d Bring the email to an end.
e Hi Kate,
f Mention the postcard you previously sent and the place visited.
g Describe the strange event in detail.

# Grammar

**So, such**

We use so and such to give emphasis. So is an adverb and we follow it with an adjective without a noun or with another adverb. We can also use so before much and many.
Such is an adjective and it is followed by another adjective and a noun or just a noun on its own. We can't use such before much or many.
*It was so peculiar that nobody could explain it.*
*She looked at me so strangely that I knew something was wrong.*
*She was missing for so many hours that we called the police.*
*This murder mystery novel is such a good book.*
*Wayne got such a fright that he almost fainted.*

> **Note:** We can replace such + a/an + adjective and noun with so + adjective + a/an + noun.
> *It was such a bizarre idea that I didn't know what to think.*
> *It was so bizarre an idea that I didn't know what to think.*

**Complete the sentences with so or such.**

1 *Enchanted* is _____ a great TV programme.
2 Harry's _____ disappointed he didn't solve the mystery.
3 The film was _____ scary that Rebecca couldn't watch it.
4 Mystery Road is located in _____ beautiful countryside.
5 I've been to Alexandria _____ many times that I don't need a map to get there.
6 It was _____ a boring detective story that I fell asleep.
7 It's strange that _____ much fuss has been made about the Yeti.
8 There was _____ a loud noise when the glass mysteriously smashed.

**Describing and recommending things**

It was the most interesting/fascinating/exciting location/event/book/film I've ever been to/read/seen.
It tells the story of/It's about…
The story/mystery begins when …
It's a place where …/It's an event that takes place …
It's such a/so … a … that …
I'd recommend it without hesitation …
I highly recommend it to …
If you enjoy …, you will love it.
It's a must for fans of …

# Writing task

*This is part of an email you received from an English-speaking friend.*

> You said you were reading a book about a mystery. What kind of mystery was it? Do you recommend it?

*Write an email answering your friend's questions.*

## Write right!

**Use these steps to help you write your email.**

**Step 1** Underline the questions in the writing task that you must answer in your email.

**Step 2** Make a list of books you have read that describe a mystery. If you haven't read any mystery books then think of a possible mystery that a book could be written about.

**Step 3** Make a note of details like the title of the book, the author's name, the main characters' names, the mystery involved.

**Step 4** Make a plan for your email. Make sure the plan includes a paragraph introducing the book, a paragraph describing the mystery and a paragraph making a recommendation. Use the plan opposite to help you.

**Step 5** Use your notes, your plan and the useful language above to write your email.

**Step 6** Edit your email to check that you have used qualifiers properly.

## Discussion

'We all need a sense of mystery in our lives.' Discuss.

# Review 6

## Vocabulary

### A Match.

1. I passed up the
2. We haven't got to the
3. It didn't cross
4. He broke into
5. He won the title
6. He isn't a follower
7. I can't draw
8. Liz has made a

a. song at the supermarket.
b. against all odds.
c. chance to meet Jason Orange.
d. my mind to wear formal dress.
e. bottom of the mystery.
f. of fashion.
g. name for herself as a writer.
h. any conclusions yet.

### B Complete the word groups.

| glory | element | seamstress |
| tambourine | tuxedo |

1. flute       accordion       _____
2. denims      bow-tie         _____
3. composer    designer        _____
4. part        aspect          _____
5. triumph     success         _____

### C Write the correct words.

| embroidered | floral | leather | plaid | velvet |

_____        _____

_____

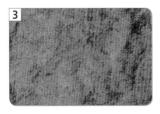

_____        _____

## D Complete the paragraph with these words.

| clarinet | composition | indication |
| lyrics | occupant | sleuth |

It had always been Tony's ambition to become a (1) _____ and so when he found himself in the middle of a mystery one day, he felt confident that he could investigate. He had gone to make his weekly delivery of groceries to an elderly neighbour and found the front door wide open. However, the (2) _____ didn't seem to be there. No one answered when he rang the bell and shouted 'hello' and there was no (3) _____ that anybody was at home. Then he heard a noise coming from upstairs. He put the shopping down and went up, calling out as he went. The noise was coming from the attic. He slowly opened the attic door and found the strangest sight he had ever seen. The lady's attic was a recording studio and she was at the window playing the (4) _____ ! 'Ah, Toby,' she said, showing no surprise at seeing him. 'I had a great idea for a song. I wrote down the (5) _____ and then I just had to come up here and work on the music! Do you want to hear my new (6) _____ ?' Toby burst out laughing. The lady's mysterious disappearance was solved.

## Grammar

### A Rearrange the words to make sentences.

1. waited / outside / the / patiently / fans
2. plays / worse / the / than / he / saxophone / you
3. made / my / hurt / noise / ears / such / he / loud / a
4. so / keep / these / off / are / big / falling / they / shoes
5. sing / song / so / don't / fast / the

**B** **The words in bold are wrong. Write the correct words.**

1 That's a **woollen, lovely, red** coat you're wearing. _____

2 That man never looks **happily**. _____

3 'Which flute do you want?' '**Neither** will do; I don't mind.' _____

4 The kids wrote the music **itself**. _____

5 What's wrong? You look **confusing**. _____

6 It took me **so** a long time to read *Suspense*. _____

**C** **Complete the paragraph with the correct form of the verbs in brackets.**

Tonight's a big night for *The Trendsetters*. The popular teen band, who (1) _____ (come) from Bolton, (2) _____ (rehearse) for months now. At nine o'clock, they (3) _____ (go) on stage. The band's drummer, Bob Wailer, (4) _____ (write) lots of new songs during the summer. *The Trendsetters* (5) _____ (not perform) these songs yet in public, so everyone (6) _____ (look forward) to hearing them. (7) _____ (you/buy) a ticket yet? If not, you'd better hurry up because it (8) _____ (be) a night to remember!

**D** **Circle the correct words.**

1 The concert hall was so / such full we couldn't get in.

2 The tour was exhausted / exhausting for the group.

3 Will nobody / somebody explain what's happening?

4 How did you cut yourself / your?

5 Fans are screaming excitedly now / now excitedly.

6 Please give Patty this guitar. It's her / hers.

7 It isn't nice criticise / to criticise others.

8 Does she dance more graceful / gracefully than you?

**Quiz time!**

What kind of music suits your personality? Do the quick quiz to find out.

1 Which tickets would you prefer?
   a tickets to a concert where lots of bands will be performing
   b tickets for a cruise
   c tickets for a play or musical

2 How loud do you like your music?
   a loud enough to be heard on the other side of town
   b quite loud
   c loud enough to listen comfortably

3 What sort of clothes are in your wardrobe?
   a black T-shirts and trousers
   b only the latest fashions
   c both fashionable and formal clothes

4 Which of these fashion accessories do you like best?
   a sunglasses
   b bags, belts and shoes
   c expensive jewellery

5 Which of these instruments do you like best?
   a the drums
   b keyboards
   c the violin

If most of your answers were a's, you like music that is popular at the moment, but not necessarily mainstream pop music. You adore rock music and alternative music, and you like to listen to it as loud as possible wherever you go so that everyone else can hear it too.

If most of your answers were b's, then you like to keep up to date with popular mainstream music. You love fun songs and you're probably very sociable.

If most of your answers were c's, then you aren't really concerned with what music is popular at the moment. You like traditional music. You prefer to listen to music being played live in concert and love watching musicians at work.

# The Olympians

## Before you watch

**A  Answer the questions with your partner.**

- Where did the first Olympic Games take place?
- Which sports do you enjoy? Are they Olympic sports?
- Do you think boxing is dangerous? Should it be stopped?
- Which do you prefer; team sports or individual sports?
- What prizes do winners of Olympic events get in the modern games?

**B  The story**

This story is set in Greece. It's about the Olympic Games, which started in 776 BC in a place called Olympia.

## Words to know

**A  Match the words to the pictures.**

boxing   discus   javelin   long jump   running   wrestling

_____  _____  _____  _____  _____  _____

**B  Match the words and phrases to the definitions.**

1  skill
2  equestrian event
3  competitor
4  opponent
5  medal
6  olive wreath

a  a person you compete against in a fight, game, etc
b  the knowledge and ability to do something well
c  a sport that involves horses
d  a circle of leaves given to the winners of Olympic events in the past
e  a person who takes part in a competition
f  a small circular piece of metal given to the winner of a competition

## While you watch

**A  Watch the video. Make notes about the changes that have occurred since the ancient Olympic Games. What sporting events did they have in the ancient games? What was the athletes' training like? How were the winners treated?**

**B  Watch again. Write T (true) or F (false).**

1  A discus thrower was the first Olympic champion.  ☐
2  Horse riding was an event in the pentathlon.  ☐
3  Boxers used to hold weights in their hands.  ☐
4  Boxing matches had no time limit.  ☐
5  Olympic winners were highly respected.  ☐
6  There were no Olympic Games for nearly 1,500 years.  ☐

**C Watch again. Put the sentences in the correct order.**

1 This material was later replaced by metals such as bronze. ☐

2 They were celebrated in a festival. ☐

3 Over the centuries, the competition became more serious. ☐

4 Athletes now receive gold, silver and bronze medals for finishing in first, second or third place. ☐

5 He was a cook, who defeated all other competitors in a foot race. ☐

6 Surprisingly, in wrestling and boxing, size and weight were not important. ☐

## After you watch

**A Choose the correct answers.**

1 The first champion, Coroebus, won his race in _____ .
   a 776 BC
   b 766 BC
   c 756 BC

2 For the ancient games, Olympic athletes had to begin training _____ before the games.
   a ten months
   b thirty days
   c ten days

3 The discus was originally made of _____ .
   a bronze
   b silver
   c stone

4 The first modern games took place in _____ .
   a 1996
   b 1896
   c 1796

**B Grammar Focus: Circle the correct words.**

1 Athletes travelled / were travelling from all over Greece to compete.

2 Chariot racing would / used to be an Olympic event.

3 Some sports focused / were focusing on strength, while others required speed.

4 The first modern Olympic Games took / were taking place in Athens.

5 Foot races would be / were the main events in the ancient games.

6 In the past, long jumpers were holding / used to hold weights in their hands.

## Project

Work alone or in small groups. Research the modern Olympic Games at the library or on the Internet. Find at least two sports that are included in the games. For each sport, find a photo, answer the questions below and add any other interesting pieces of information you find. Make a chart and present it to the whole class.

### Olympic Sport Information: Bobsleighing

1 What is the sport? Is it a team or individual sport?
_____
_____

2 What equipment does it need?
_____
_____

3 Where is it played?
_____
_____

4 What do you like most about this sport?
_____
_____

# The Adventure Capital of the World

## Before you watch

**A   Answer the questions with your partner.**

- Have you ever tried an adventure sport?
- Would you like to try bungee jumping? Why? Why not?
- What is the most frightening thing you have done?
- How much do you know about New Zealand?
- Why do you think Queenstown is called the Adventure Capital of the World?

**B   The story**

This story is set in New Zealand, in a place called Queenstown. It is a centre for adventure sports, attracting people from all over the world.

**New Zealand**
**Queenstown**

## Words to know

**Match the words to the definitions.**

| | | | |
|---|---|---|---|
| 1 | adventure | a | a long walk in a natural area |
| 2 | bridge | b | any of the activities you do in your free time |
| 3 | bungee jumping | c | something that is not deep |
| 4 | hike | d | any experience which is exciting and dangerous |
| 5 | pastime | e | a sport in which people jump from a high place with a special rope |
| 6 | propeller | f | a vehicle that rises straight up into the air and flies across an area |
| 7 | shallow | g | a structure used to cross a river |
| 8 | helicopter | h | a device which pushes a boat or aircraft forward |

## While you watch

**A   Watch the video. Make notes about Queenstown, its scenery and the activities you can do there, so you can describe them to your partner.**

**B   Watch again. Write T (true) or F (false).**

1   Queenstown is a quiet place. ☐
2   Jetboats were invented in New Zealand. ☐
3   Jetboats are designed for use in shallow water. ☐
4   A new adventure involves a 60-day hike on a mountain. ☐
5   A helicopter takes hikers to the top of the mountain. ☐
6   Adventure sports are good for tourism in New Zealand. ☐

**C   Watch again. Circle the words you hear.**

1   If you like thrilling / exciting adventure sports, New Zealand is the place to do them.
2   Riding in a jetboat is a shallow / special experience.
3   Jetboats are also really good at giving customers a(n) adventure / thrill.
4   This is one of the number-one pastimes / activities of people coming to New Zealand.
5   High wire bungee and bridge bungee are both thrilling and slightly commercial / frightening sports.
6   The people who have to really try hard / lean forward to jump are the ones that get the most out of it.

# After you watch

**A Choose the correct answers.**

1 The bungee jumpers dive about _____ metres.
   a  34
   b  134
   c  440

2 _____ were especially designed for New Zealand's shallow rivers.
   a  Adventure sports
   b  Jetboats
   c  Helicopters

3 People who hike up the mountain _____ back to Queenstown after about ten to fifteen minutes at the top.
   a  fly
   b  hike
   c  walk

4 The _____ at Kawarau was the world's first commercial bungee jumping site.
   a  bridge
   b  birthplace
   c  mountain

**B Grammar Focus: Circle the correct words.**

1 We have hiked / been hiking up this mountain for three hours.

2 There are many people which / who don't enjoy adventure sports.

3 She decided that bungee jumping was frightening enough / too frightening for her to try.

4 They had to walk back down the mountain as they had been missing / missed the helicopter ride back into Queenstown.

5 This was the first time he had ridden / been riding in a jetboat.

6 Henry Van Asch, who / that works at Queenstown, says bungee jumping is very popular.

## Project

**Imagine you visited Queenstown in New Zealand for an adventure holiday. Write an e-mail to your friend telling them about which sport or sports you did and how it made you feel. Mention any other adventure sports that you would like to try.**

Email
New    Reply    Forward    Print    Delete

Dear _____ ,

_____

_____

_____

_____

_____

_____

_____

Bye for now!

_____

# One Boy's Journey

## Before you watch

**A** **Answer the questions with your partner.**

- How much do you know about cattle? What do they eat? What do we use them for?
- What do you think the landscape and the weather is like in the Sahel, a region near the Sahara?
- How do you think most people who live there earn their living?
- What is the longest journey you have ever been on?
- What are some of the difficulties of travelling long distances?

**B** **The story**

This story is set in the African countries of Mali and Mauritania, in a region called the Sahel, a long, narrow band of dry land at the southern edge of the Sahara.

**Northern Africa**
**Diafarabe, Mali**

## Words to know

**A** **Match the words and phrases to the definitions.**

| | | | |
|---|---|---|---|
| 1 | arid | a | people who steal cows and bulls |
| 2 | cattle | b | not very hot and not very cold |
| 3 | cattle rustlers | c | large farm animals kept for their milk or meat |
| 4 | dairy cows | d | wild animals from Africa and Asia that look like dogs |
| 5 | grazing | e | people who are fighting against their own government |
| 6 | herdsmen | f | cows used for producing milk |
| 7 | hyenas | g | having little water or rain, very dry |
| 8 | mosquitoes | h | eating grass and other plants growing in a field |
| 9 | rebels | i | men or boys who care for groups of animals such as cows |
| 10 | temperate | j | small flying insects which bite people and animals and suck their blood |

## While you watch

**A** **Watch the video. Tick (✓) the dangers of the journey mentioned in the video.**

1 dairy cows ☐
2 mosquitoes ☐
3 herdsmen ☐
4 hyenas ☐
5 cattle rustlers ☐
6 the river ☐

**B** **Watch again. Put the sentences in the correct order.**

1 Aissa hopes that Yoro has done well. ☐
2 He chooses to cross the river with them to ensure their safety. ☐
3 They make this dangerous journey for one reason: to feed their cattle. ☐
4 If a Fulani boy returns with healthy cattle, then he is considered to be a man. ☐
5 Putting his brand on the calves is a proud moment for Yoro. ☐
6 After three months in the bush, it's finally time for Yoro to turn and go home. ☐

**C Watch again. Circle the words you hear.**

1 Soon it will be too rainy / wet in the delta.

2 The Sahel is an arid region with very few rivers / plants and trees.

3 'In the bush / desert we have to be completely focused.'

4 The other Fulani people will look carefully / closely at the cattle.

5 Fulani families / parents choose who their daughters and sons marry.

6 Night-time is when the rebels / hyenas come out.

# After you watch

**A Choose the correct answers.**

1 Cattle usually prefer a _____ climate to a dry one.
  a    wet
  b    temperate
  c    arid

2 Yoro Sisse is away from home for about _____ .
  a    3 months
  b    6 months
  c    8 months

3 The young herdsmen live mainly on _____ during their journey.
  a    meat
  b    milk
  c    water

4 The route Yoro takes on his journey is _____ .
  a    ancient
  b    short
  c    new

**B Grammar Focus: Circle the correct words.**

1 Yoro must leave the Niger Delta because it will be too wet / wet enough to stay.

2 Sometimes the herdsmen can / have to stay up all night to protect their cattle.

3 By the time Yoro returns to his village he will be / have been away from home for several months.

4 At the end of the dry season, young Fulani tribesmen set out / are setting out on their long journey to find grazing for their cattle.

5 Some mosquitoes can / must cause serious diseases.

6 Aissa is pleased / pleasing that Yoro is coming home.

## Project

Cattle farming is a major part of the farming industry. Think of some other important types of farming that exist. Some examples are sheep farming and vegetable farming. Write a short paragraph about what life is like for a farmer. Describe some of the challenges, then explain what you imagine would be some benefits of having a farm.

**Our farm**

_____

_____

_____

_____

_____

_____

_____

# Wind Power

USA, Iowa
Spirit Lake

## Before you watch

**A  Answer the questions with your partner.**

- How many sources of energy can you name?
- Which of those energy sources are better for the environment?
- What sort of climate does your country have?
- How much do you know about wind power?
- What alternative sources of energy are used in your country?

**B  The story**

This story is set in Spirit Lake, Iowa, in the United States. It is about a school district that has found a way to save money and help the environment.

## Words to know

**A  Match the words to the pictures.**

> crops    foundation    silos    steel rods    wind turbine

| 1 | 2 | 3 | 4 | 5 |
|---|---|---|---|---|

_____    _____    _____    _____    _____

**B  Match the words and phrases to the definitions.**

| | | | |
|---|---|---|---|
| 1 | blades | a | coal or oil, for example |
| 2 | efficient | b | the centre of something that spins |
| 3 | fossil fuel | c | able to handle the force of something without breaking |
| 4 | hub | d | thin, wide pieces of metal or plastic attached to a centre that spins |
| 5 | withstand | e | an area that contains schools |
| 6 | school district | f | able to do something without wasting time or resources |

## While you watch

**A  Watch the video. Make notes about the economic and environmental advantages wind power has brought to Spirit Lake. When you have finished, compare your notes with your partner's.**

**B  Watch again. Write T (true) or F (false).**

1  The countryside around Spirit Lake is hilly. ☐
2  The wind turbines are saving the schools lots of money. ☐
3  Iowa sometimes gets tornadoes. ☐
4  The smaller turbine sends its power to Des Moines. ☐
5  Farmers are against having wind turbines on their land. ☐
6  Jan Bolluyt teaches biology. ☐

**C  Watch again. Circle the words you hear.**

1  From the inside, it's clear just how tall / big the turbines really are.

2  In extremely strong winds, the huge blades / propellers of the wind turbines simply shut down.

3  The schools aren't the only ones who are making money in the power / energy business.

4  Farmer Charles Goodman thinks he'll make an extra $6,000 / $16,000 a year from the three turbines on his farm.

5  These turbines provide enough electricity / energy to power a city like Des Moines.

6  They write down the amounts of fossil fuels, such as oil / coal, that are no longer needed for energy for the school.

# After you watch

**A  Choose the correct answers.**

1  The first wind turbine in Spirit Lake was built in _____ .
a  1973
b  1983
c  1993

2  The two turbines could save the district $140,000 a _____ in energy costs.
a  week
b  month
c  year

3  The turbines can produce energy from winds of _____ miles an hour.
a  eight
b  eighteen
c  eighty

4  As well as making money from selling their _____ , farmers also make money from the wind.
a  crops
b  silos
c  fields

**B  Grammar Focus: Circle the correct words.**

1  I wish more people would / had use wind power.

2  The neighbours have / are having wind turbines set up in their garden.

3  Global warming will get worse unless we will stop / stop cutting down forests.

4  If they hadn't installed wind turbines and saved money, the Spirit Lake School District wouldn't have / hadn't been able to employ more teachers.

5  Some farmers have allowed energy companies building / to build wind turbines right next to their fields.

6  If the wind is too strong, the turbines are shutting down / shut down.

## Project

**Work in pairs or small groups. Find out what you can about different ways of producing energy. Choose one and make a poster which explains how it works, how it saves money, where it can be built and how it helps the environment. Find photos to illustrate your poster. Present the poster to the class, explaining the information on it.**

**WIND IS IN!**

- Wind power is made from building wind turbines that use wind to make power.

- When wind passes through a wind turbine, it makes the blades of the turbine spin. Energy is made inside the turbine, and this energy can be used to power homes.

- Wind turbines can be built anywhere there is space for them. They can be built in open fields, on the tops of hills and on the sides of mountains. They can even be built in cities. They don't have to be built near homes, though, as power made from wind turbines can be sent far away.

- Wind power is very clean, unlike fossil fuels that pollute the air. It is also cheap, as wind exists everywhere and we will never run out of it. There will always be wind on our planet.

# Butler School

England

## Before you watch

**A  Answer the questions with your partner.**

- What do butlers do? What are some of their duties?
- What sort of people do you think become butlers?
- What sort of people do they work for?
- Are there many butlers in the world today?
- How do people become butlers?

**B  The story**

This story takes place in England, at the Ivor Spencer International School for Butler Administrators. Men and women from many countries come here to learn the skills a butler needs.

## Words to know

**A  Match the words to the definitions.**

| | | | |
|---|---|---|---|
| 1 | ambassador | a | a polite term for a man, used to show respect |
| 2 | butler | b | to finish a course of studies at a school |
| 3 | gentleman | c | to get something for someone and bring it to them |
| 4 | graduate | d | an important official who represents their government while living outside their country |
| 5 | lord | e | the chief servant in the house of a wealthy family |
| 6 | fetch | f | the title of a man who is very important |

**B  Complete the sentences with these words.**

> appreciate    certificate    improvement    introduce    refreshments    title

1  When the guests arrive, David will _____ himself as the butler of the house.
2  In England, many people have _____ such as tea and sandwiches at five o'clock in the afternoon.
3  A word such as 'Mr', 'Dr' or 'Sir' before a name is a _____ .
4  When you successfully finish a course of study or training you get a _____ to prove it.
5  John said he would _____ some help with his project.
6  Learning how to be a butler is difficult at first, but after some practice, most show signs of _____ .

## While you watch

**A  Watch the video. Tick (✓) the things the butlers must learn.**

| | | | | |
|---|---|---|---|---|
| 1 | How to iron a newspaper | ☐ | 4  How to walk correctly | ☐ |
| 2 | How to speak English | ☐ | 5  How to stop a thief | ☐ |
| 3 | How to use computers | ☐ | 6  How to cook | ☐ |

**B  Watch again. Put the sentences into the correct order.**

1  Butlers must also learn how to recognise quality products, or 'the finer things in life'.  ☐
2  Over the next five weeks, 13 international students will have 86 lessons in the art of being a butler.  ☐
3  Every real gentleman had servants, especially a butler.  ☐
4  Before they came here, these young men and women drove buses, worked with computers, or worked in restaurants or shops.  ☐
5  So where does one find a good butler nowdays?  ☐
6  For example, they might need to deal with unwelcome guests.  ☐

146

**C Watch again. Circle the words you hear.**

1 Long ago, England was a land of country houses, palaces, castles / gardens and afternoon tea.
2 A proper / real butler must learn how to carry himself correctly.
3 'We know you've come from all over the world and we recognise / appreciate you being here.'
4 It's important for gentlemen / students to keep their hopes up and practise, practise, practise!
5 There are a lot of qualities / secrets to being a good butler.
6 If you see a(n) burnt / ironed newspaper, you know the butler's very interested.

# After you watch

**A Choose the correct answers.**

1 Today there are fewer than _____ butlers in England.
  a 70
  b 200
  c 30,000

2 On every course there are about _____ people who don't make it past the first two days.
  a 2
  b 5
  c 13

3 Future butlers must learn how to use the correct _____ to refer to ambassadors and other important people.
  a names
  b words
  c titles

4 What language does the word 'butler' come from?
  a English
  b French
  c Spanish

**B Grammar Focus: Circle the correct words.**

1 At the school, students are taught / teaching how to carry themselves correctly.
2 The butler said that he will / would bring the guest's car immediately.
3 David said he learned / had learned a lot during the course.
4 He phoned his girlfriend and said / told her that he was enjoying his studies.
5 He also said that he missed / is missing his family and friends.
6 When a student has completed the course successfully, they are given / being given a certificate.

## Project

Work alone or in small groups. Use your imagination to make a poster advertising a new butler school or another school that teaches an interesting job or skill (eg cooking, language skills, hair styling etc). Use photos to illustrate your advertisement. Write information about what course is available, what students will learn and appreciate about the course and how long it will be. Don't forget to include a start date and meeting place for the course and a telephone number for people to find out more information.

## Traditional Butler School

Would you like to learn about the finer things in life? Perhaps you would like to work for a king? Take our butler training course and learn the art of being a butler.

Being a butler requires much skill and knowledge. In our course you will learn how to carry yourself properly, entertain at parties and recognise quality products. You will learn all of this in just four weeks.

Our next butler training course begins on 2 February at the Traditional Butler School, 170 Campden St, London. Call 00 99 41 00 for more information.

Join us for an enjoyable experience learning the art of being a butler!

# The Lost Temples of the Maya

**Guatemala**
El Mirador

## Before you watch

**A  Answer the questions with your partner.**

- Where is Guatemala?
- What do you think the landscape and weather are like there?
- What do you know about archaeology?
- What do you know about pyramids?
- How many ancient civilizations do you know about?

**B  The story**

This story is set in Guatemala, a country in Central America. It takes place in the lost city of El Mirador, where archaeologists are digging for clues to the early Maya kings.

## Words to know

**A  Match the words to the definitions.**

| | | | |
|---|---|---|---|
| 1 | buried | a | the foot of an animal such as a tiger |
| 2 | civilization | b | placed in the ground |
| 3 | evidence | c | the culture and society of a people |
| 4 | paw | d | a special place where a dead person is put |
| 5 | ruins | e | the remains of very old buildings |
| 6 | tomb | f | anything that makes you believe something is true or exists |

**B  Complete the sentences with these words.**

> dig    jungle    mystery    platform    region    temple

1  The archaeologist is preparing to _____ at another pyramid next year.
2  A _____ is a place where people go to pray to their gods.
3  For more than 20 years he has been trying to understand the _____ of the early Maya.
4  The ancient building rests on a _____ that is over thirty metres wide.
5  The Mayan pyramids are found in the thick _____ of Guatemala.
6  The _____ of southern Mexico and Central America has got many Mayan ruins.

## While you watch

**A  Watch the video. Make notes about what you see at the archaeological dig. What kind of equipment do they use? What is the site like? Do archaeologists work in teams, or alone? When you have finished, compare your notes with your partner's.**

**B  Watch again. Put the sentences into the correct order.**

1  The Danta pyramid was built during a time that many people consider to be basic and simple.  ☐
2  This special equipment sends electrical currents through the ground.  ☐
3  During that time, he has been trying to solve the mystery of the early Maya.  ☐
4  One of the stones in the pyramid has a large jaguar paw with three claws on it.  ☐
5  He still feels that they're real and he's not content to give up easily.  ☐
6  The team could be just a few minutes away from finding the tomb of 'Great Fiery Jaguar Paw'.  ☐

**C  Watch again. Circle the words you hear.**

1   Under the branches / leaves and earth of the Guatemalan jungle, the secrets of this new discovery may lie under one of the biggest pyramids ever built.
2   They may be near an ancient city that has been lost for hundreds / thousands of years.
3   Hansen hopes to find the answers by exploring / digging under the pyramids.
4   He hopes that their tombs / temples will reveal who they were.
5   The system then creates an image / a map of what's under the soil.
6   Maybe he will finally find what he's looking for in the lost ruins / temples of the Maya.

# After you watch

**A  Choose the correct answers.**

1   Archaeologists are now discovering a Mayan civilisation that existed _____ years before the Classic Period.
    a   10,000
    b   1,000
    c   100

2   The pyramid of Danta is the _____ pyramid at El Mirador.
    a   tallest
    b   most complex
    c   largest

3   Hansen believes that the jaguar paw is the _____ of a Mayan king.
    a   object
    b   symbol
    c   animal

4   The open space they found under the pyramid was _____ metres under the earth.
    a   11
    b   8
    c   22

**B  Grammar Focus: Circle the correct words.**

1   The jaguar is much larger / largest than an ordinary cat.
2   Guatemala is in Central America, is it / isn't it?
3   Hansen believes that the jaguar paw, with its / it's three claws, is evidence of a king's tomb.
4   He hopes that by this time next year he has found / will have found the king's tomb.
5   The Guatemalan jungle must be the more / most interesting place he's ever seen.
6   The archaeologists had been digging / had dug for three days before they found anything.

## Project

Imagine you visited a Mayan ruin in Guatemala. Write a postcard to your friend telling them about what you saw, what you did there and how much you enjoyed it.

Dear _____ ,

_____

_____

_____

_____

_____

_____

See you soon,

_____

GUATEMALA 5

40 Penbroke Street
Fulham, London
NW1
England

# Irregular verbs

| Infinitive | Past Simple | Past Participle |
|---|---|---|
| be | was/were | been |
| become | became | become |
| begin | began | begun |
| bend | bent | bent |
| bite | bit | bitten |
| break | broke | broken |
| bring | brought | brought |
| build | built | built |
| burn | burnt | burnt |
| buy | bought | bought |
| can | could | – |
| catch | caught | caught |
| choose | chose | chosen |
| come | came | come |
| cost | cost | cost |
| cut | cut | cut |
| deal | dealt | dealt |
| do | did | done |
| draw | drew | drawn |
| dream | dreamt | dreamt |
| drink | drank | drunk |
| drive | drove | driven |
| eat | ate | eaten |
| fall | fell | fallen |
| feed | fed | fed |
| feel | felt | felt |
| fight | fought | fought |
| find | found | found |
| fly | flew | flown |
| forecast | forecast | forecast |
| forget | forgot | forgotten |
| get | got | got |
| give | gave | given |
| go | went | gone |
| grow | grew | grown |
| have | had | had |
| hear | heard | heard |
| hide | hid | hidden |
| hit | hit | hit |
| hold | held | held |
| hurt | hurt | hurt |
| keep | kept | kept |
| know | knew | known |
| lead | led | led |
| learn | learnt | learnt |
| leave | left | left |
| lend | lent | lent |
| let | let | let |

| Infinitive | Past Simple | Past Participle |
|---|---|---|
| lie | lay | lain |
| lose | lost | lost |
| mean | meant | meant |
| make | made | made |
| meet | met | met |
| pay | paid | paid |
| put | put | put |
| read | read [red] | read [red] |
| ride | rode | ridden |
| ring | rang | rung |
| rise | rose | risen |
| run | ran | run |
| say | said | said |
| see | saw | seen |
| sell | sold | sold |
| send | sent | sent |
| set | set | set |
| shake | shook | shaken |
| shine | shone | shone |
| show | showed | shown |
| shoot | shot | shot |
| shut | shut | shut |
| sing | sang | sung |
| sink | sank | sunk |
| sit | sat | sat |
| sleep | slept | slept |
| slide | slid | slid |
| smell | smelt | smelt |
| speak | spoke | spoken |
| speed | sped | sped |
| spend | spent | spent |
| split | split | split |
| stand | stood | stood |
| steal | stole | stolen |
| stick | stuck | stuck |
| stink | stank | stunk |
| sweep | swept | swept |
| swim | swam | swum |
| take | took | taken |
| teach | taught | taught |
| tell | told | told |
| think | thought | thought |
| throw | threw | thrown |
| understand | understood | understood |
| wear | wore | worn |
| win | won | won |
| write | wrote | written |

**Wonderful World 6 Pupil's Book**
Katrina Gormley

Publisher: Jason Mann

Director of Content Development: Sarah Bideleux

Development Editor: Lynn Thomson

Assistant Editor: Manuela Barros

Content Project Editor: Amy Smith

Art Director: Natasa Arsenidou

Cover Designer: Vasiliki Christoforidou

Text Designers: Natasa Arsenidou

Compositor: Dora Danasi

National Geographic Editorial Liaison: Leila Hishmeh

**Acknowledgements**

Illustrated by Theodoros Piakis
Recorded at Motivation Sound Studios and GFS-PRO Studio
Production at GFS-PRO Studio by George Flamouridis

The publisher would like to thank the following sources for permission to reproduce their copyright protected photos:
**Dreamtime DLL** – pp. 8 (Denis Makarenko), 115 (Gianpirex), 128 (Sandra Dragojlovic), 138 (Piotr Sikora); **Fotolia** – pp. 23 (Mytho, kmiragaya), 26 (Corbis), 63 (Liv Friis-larsen), 66 (Alx); **iStockphoto** – pp. 16–17 (Yory Frenklakh). **National Geographic** – pp. 28–29 (Michael Melford), 60–61 (Gordon Wiltsie); **Shutterstock** – pp. 5 (Fesus Robert, Katarzyna Krawiec, Naturaldigital, Studiotouch, Emin Ozkan, Elnur), 8 (Andrejs Pidjass, debra hughes), 9 (Thomas Barrat), 13 (RoxyFer, Tatiana Morozova, bikeriderlondon, Petrenko Andriy), 14 (Elpis Ioannidis, Andrey Lukashenkov), 18 (Pokaz), 21 (sculpies), 22 (markrhiggins, Karen Hadley, @erics, Alexander Dvorak, Frederick R. Matzen, Daniel Yordano, Olga Sapegina, Kheng Guan Toh), 23 (Mecc, LOURDU PRAKASH XAVIER, Vladimir Wrange, Laurence Gough), 26 (mvp23, steamroller_blues, Harald Høiland Tjøstheim, WitR), 30 (Nihat Dursun), 34 (Stéphane Bidouze, Andreea S.), 35 (sculpies, Gorilla, Lisa F. Young, Geir Olav Lyngfjell, Galyna Andrushko, Morgan Lane Photography), 40 (PHOTOCREO Michal Bednarek) 43 (Cynthia Farmer, Evgeniapp, elwynn,, Andriy Solovyov, Suzanne Tucker, jamalludin), 44 (Denis Babenko), 46 (pixelman), 49 (Kapu, GRISHA), 56 (Rob Wilson, LeCajun), 57 (Michael Pettigrew, Maksim Toome, XAOC, ilker canikligil, ArchMan), 58 (Sanevich), 62 (Kiselev Andrey Valerevich), 64 (Zurijeta), 65 (Joe Gough, marilyn barbone, Aaron Amat, GalaxyPhoto, Kwong Yiing Woan, Stephen VanHorn, niderlander), 67 (Mrs.Blondy), 68 (Jag_cz, Lisovskaya Natalia), 70 (Don Tran, Johann Piber, Sailorr, James Steidl, Estea, pandapaw, 6493866629), 78 (Galyna Andrushko), 79 (Jose AS Reyes, Mikhail Olykainen, Julija Sapic, Caitlin Mirra, Galyna Andrushko), 84 (Stephen Gibson, STILLFX), 85 (justin maresch, ilker canikligil, jeff Metzger, HomeStudio, Jeremy Smith, Christopher Meder - Photography), 86 (Stubblefield Photography), 87 (ANATOL, Amy Walters, BonD80, stocksnapp, Andrey Yurlov), 92 (Anyka, ollirg, ason, r.martens, 3d brained), 96 (Dmitriy Shironosov, Nataliia Natykach, Marcin Balcerzak), 100 (JoLin, Steve Cukrov, Susan Law Cain, Steve Cukrov, nostal6ie), 101 (michaeljung, Lisa F. Young, Dwight Smith), 106 (Victor Newman, Monkey Business Images, dusko, Christophe Testi), 107 (remik44992, dadek, Monkey Business Images, Vuk Vukmirovic), 110 (Aleksandr Kurganov, Andresr), 114 (Rob Marmion, Christina Richards, Brian Weed, Thomas SkjÃ?Â¦veland, iBird), 116–117 (RoxyFer), 119 (Karkas), 123 (Thomas M Perkins, Ronald Sumners, John Blanton, Thomas M Perkins, carlo dapino, eAlisa, Jaimie Duplass), 131 (Alexander Chaikin, Tomas Sereda), 137 (grynold), 138 (Phase4Photography, mjones), 139 (Steve Broer), 140 (jan kranendonk), 141 (Kapu), 142 (Richard Williamson), 144 (Zastol`skiy Victor Leonidovich, Gilles Lougassi, Noam Armonn, BelleMedia, Jorg Hackemann), 145 (Brian A Jackson), 147 (Peter Clark), 149 (Nataliya Hora); Thinkstock – pp. 23 (Hemera), 24 (Hemera Technologies), 26 (iStockphoto), 40 (iStockphoto), 53 (iStockphoto), 57 (Ciaran Griffin/Stockbyte), 100 (Photos.com), 101 (iStockphoto), 122 (Photos.com/Jupiterimages), 138 (Photos.com/Jupiterimages).

Printed in Greece by Bakis SA
Print Number 08 Print Year 2016

ISBN: 978-1-111-40257-0

**National Geographic Learning**
Cheriton House
North Way
Andover
Hampshire
SP10 5BE
United Kingdom

Cengage Learning is a leading provider of customized learning solutions with office locations around the globe, including Singapore, the United Kingdom, Australia, Mexico, Brazil and Japan. Locate your local office at:
**international.cengage.com/region**

Cengage Learning products are represented in Canada by Nelson Education, Ltd.

Visit National Geographic Learning online at **ngl.cengage.com**

Visit our corporate website at **www.cengage.com**